Praise for *The A*

"If you have ever wondered what evolution has to do with faith, hope, love, and forgiveness, start here. In meditations both bold and beautiful, Bruce Sanguin shows us how new Christian faith can look in the age of science."
—John F. Haught, senior fellow of science and religion at the Woodstock Theological Center

"By deftly bridging the evidence-based revelation of science with the premodern beauty of scripture, Bruce Sanguin persuades us that evolution and Christianity can be allies in the advance of love."
—Michael Dowd, author of *Thank God for Evolution* (endorsed by six Nobel laureate scientists)

"Bruce Sanguin's *Advance of Love* is a significant gift to evolutionary spirituality. Packed full of important spiritual truths, *The Advance of Love* clearly demonstrates that the Bible remains a potent force, even within a 'post-postmodern' perspective. Bruce's sermons are both thoughtful and inspiring, and will serve as a spiritual tonic for all who read them. I highly recommend all of Bruce's wonderful work."
—Steve McIntosh, author of *Evolution's Purpose* and *Integral Consciousness and the Future of Evolution*

"In *The Advance of Love*, Bruce Sanguin's challenging reflections burn with evolutionary hope. They are also likely to push the religious comfort zone of many. . . Thank goodness!"
—Rex A E Hunt, chair of Common Dreams: A Conference of Religious Progressives in Australia and the South Pacific

"Bruce Sanguin speaks from the heart of evolution expressing through the heart of Christ. Not only does he 'read the Bible with an evolutionary heart' in *The Advance of Love*, he lives it through his words and life. He is a great minister of the conscious evolution of humanity."
—Barbara Marx Hubbard, president of the Foundation for Conscious Evolution

"*The Advance of Love* is a bright, smart, beautifully done book about Integral Christianity based specifically on the Integral Model. This is exactly the type of thinking that religious and spiritual thought needs to encounter in the coming years in order to become in sync with the modern and postmodern world, and allow Christianity (among others) to continue to thrive in a meaningful fashion. Highly recommended!"

—Ken Wilber, author of *Integral Spirituality*

The Advance of Love

For Marilyn,
My friend + one
who is giving
her life to the
advance of love.

Much gratitude,

Bruce.

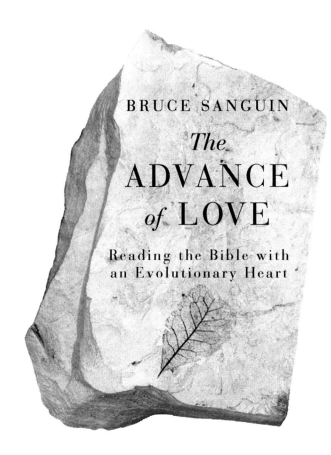

BRUCE SANGUIN

The
ADVANCE
of LOVE

Reading the Bible with
an Evolutionary Heart

Evans and Sanguin Publishing, Vancouver

Also by Bruce Sanguin:
If Darwin Prayed: Prayers for Evolutionary Mystics
The Emerging Church: A Model for Change & a Map for Renewal
Darwin, Divinity, and the Dance of the Cosmos: An Ecological Christianity
Summoning the Whirlwind: Unconventional Sermons for a Relevant Christian Faith

Scripture selections throughout are from the New Revised Standard Version of the Bible.

Evans and Sanguin Publishing
1826 West 15th Avenue
Vancouver, B.C. V6J 2M3

Library and Archives Canada Cataloguing in Publication

Sanguin, Bruce, 1955–
The advance of love : reading the Bible with an
evolutionary heart / Bruce Sanguin.

Includes bibliographical references.
Issued also in electronic format.
ISBN 978-0-9865924-3-0

1. Evolution (Biology)—Religious aspects—Christianity.
2. Bible and evolution. 3. Religion and science. I. Title.

BS659.S26 2012   231.7'652   C2012-901476-1

Cover graphic by David Drummond, salamanderhill.com
Design and layout by Bartosz Barczak

16 15 14 13 12   1 2 3 4 5

To obtain digital or print copies of this book, please visit IfDarwinPrayed.com.

For the good people of
Canadian Memorial United Church
and Centre for Peace

Is evolution a theory, a system or a hypothesis? It is much more: it is a general condition to which all theories, all hypotheses, all systems must bow and which they must satisfy henceforward if they are to be thinkable and true. Evolution is a light illuminating all facts, a curve that all lines must follow.

—Pierre Teilhard de Chardin,
The Phenomenon of Man

Contents

Preface: The Big Story

I've always been a sucker for the Big Story—the story that tells us where we came from, what life is for, and offers a glimpse into where we might be headed. The Big Story is out of fashion in our postmodern culture. Academics have noticed that this grand narrative has a tendency to privilege the dominant class, to present "reality" and "truth" from an elitist vantage point. For example, the cultural narrative of male privilege (patriarchy) has managed to construe reality in such a way that women are only now, after ten thousand years, embracing their dignity and exercising their voices. I can't argue with the critique.

Still, I don't live well without a Big Story. For the past thirty years or so, I've wrestled with, and been blessed by, the biblical narrative as one example of a Big Story. It has many limitations, to be sure. It's hard work reinterpreting and reframing the implicit assumptions of a male sky-God and the patriarchy "He" presides over. The Bible is a premodern library of books that reflect the assumptions and worldviews of its premodern writers.

Yet, for all its limitations, the Bible has its merits. For example, it is unique in that the stories are told from the perspective of the marginalized. One empire after another treated the Jewish people as little more than an asterisk in the annals of history—at best, as nuisances and nobodies—and the Bible is a record of these left-behinds, telling a story that God was with *them*. The New Testament story of

Jesus picks up on this countercultural theme, making the subversive claim that the "Son of God" was not Caesar but a Jewish backwater peasant from Galilee. When the Bible is read as a whole, one can see the progression of religious traditions that are both honoured and yet transcended. In other words, the Bible displays critical perspective on its own narrative. Finally, unlike in some religious traditions, the Bible affirms the dignity of natural and human history as an arena in which God is active, alluring all creation toward a promise of fulfilment.

This latter affirmation opens up Scripture to a dialogue with another Big Story that science has discovered. The story of evolution provides a *con*text for all sacred texts, including the Judeo-Christian narrative. It also suggests that natural and human history is moving toward increased complexity, unity, and consciousness. Some call this the Common Story of Creation. Catholic priest and geologian Thomas Berry says that it is a new sacred myth for modernist and postmodernist culture. It is not "common" as in mundane, but rather it is the foundational narrative that connects all religious lineages, as well as atheists and secular humanists alike. Everything emerged from a common origin 13.7 billion years ago and shares this singular lineage. The Common Story of Creation has a distinct advantage over earlier, mythic stories in that it is supported by science. This evolutionary narrative is accepted as foundational for every scientific discipline: cosmology, biology, quantum physics, systems theory, chaos theory, and psychology, to name a few. It isn't the role of scientists to interpret the facts from a theological viewpoint or generate a new myth for the twenty-first century. It is the role of theologians to incorporate and interpret what scientists are discovering into a New Story. We do so in fear and trembling, as scientific "facts" won't hold still. New research elicits new "facts" all the time.

Nevertheless, evolution itself seems to be as close to scientific fact as we're ever going to get. Evolution's engine is up for debate; Darwin's theory of natural selection is still the frontrunner, but there are many other theories being researched and being taken seriously by scientists. When brilliant scientists, such as Richard Dawkins, make claims that a human being is little more than a vehicle for the perpetuation of selfish genes, he's interpreting the facts by telling his own Big Story. That's fine, if he's willing to step outside his role as scientist and transparently assume the role of storyteller.

I do not interpret the evolutionary process as a meaningless series of accidents, devoid of direction, as the muscular atheists of our day suggest. Rather, it enjoys the quality of any drama, within which we expect chance and tragedy, theme and coherence, and the promise of a satisfying ending. Like with any drama, if we knew the ending ahead of time, the story could not sustain our interest. What is unique about this unfolding story is that after 13.7 billion years of evolution, we have become co-creators of the script. Whatever we mean by "God" cannot episodically intervene in this evolutionary drama to override our choices. This God's only power is the power of what process philosopher and mathematician A.N. Whitehead calls the non-coercive presence of Love.[1] As this presence of Love, God can influence (but not interfere), advancing in, through, and as us.

This book is a collection of reflections that emerged when these two stories—the Bible and evolution—were used as interpretive keys to unlock the other's deeper meaning. On the one hand, the Bible suggests a universe that is sacred in its origins and purposefulness, and that it has a Heart. On the other hand, the science of evolution allows us to interpret our ancient texts in the light of new evidence about reality. The evolutionary story updates the premodern worldview of Scripture. When the Bible and science differ on the facts, science wins. But when scientists, philosophers, and theologians differ on the interpretation of these facts, the Bible's intuition of meaning, purpose, and a biased historical trajectory gives theologians a valid perspective.

---

[1] A.N. Whitehead, *Adventures of Ideas* (Toronto: The Free Press, 1967).

As a storyteller, I image evolution as the miraculous, awe-inspiring emergence of a universe from the Heart and Mind of Reality ("God"). This combination of Heart (Love) and this Mind (Wisdom) is the milieu from which the world is endlessly and perpetually emerging—it did not just emerge 13.7 billion years ago, but rather it is emerging in every moment. Scientists call this cosmogenesis, the perpetual creativity of the universe. Evolution has been the long, slow emergence of life from matter, of conscious self-awareness from life, and now, of creatures who are able to *consciously* evolve. In us, natural selection has become actual selection.

Because everything is emerging out of Heart and Mind, I am telling a sacred story. Heart and Mind is realizing itself through this incredible adventure of diversity that we call life. To understand the story in this manner is to awaken to an essential identity, a mystic unity with All That Is. We are That which we are seeking—manifestations of the originating Mind and Heart, evolving. We are one with the Being of God and one with the Becoming of God—this emergent universe in its diverse and radiant splendour. Heart and Mind require this magnificent diversity even to approximate divine beauty.

These reflections were written out of this way of imagining the universe and this interpretive lens. Of course, it's only one of many ways to tell the story. But I'm at a place in my life when the story that I commit to must confer maximum dignity upon the cosmos, Earth, Her creatures, and the human species. Anything less doesn't resonate with the part of me that I call my soul.

I have come to imagine this evolving miracle as the advance of Love. "Love is patient," as Saint Paul wrote in his famous love letter. Love cannot coerce, but only allure. It has taken this allurement 13.7 billion years to arrive at us, and it's far from finished. "It does not insist on its own way." Love must make room by emptying itself of coercive power in order to allow genuine diversity to flourish. It "bears all things" and "endures all things." Evolution is full of cataclysms, crises, and much suffering. But can we imagine that this is what Love must also bear and endure if it is to be realized in the manifest realm of a universe—that the suffering of Jesus is an occasion of this cosmic truth? "Love never ends." Love will rise up again and again, a resurrection of Reality, because this is the nature of the divine milieu in which we live and move and have our being (1 Corinthians 13:4–8).

Paul's love letter continues telling the story of Love's advance in his own life: "When I was a child, I spoke like a child, I thought like a child, I reasoned like a child; when I became an adult, I put an end to childish ways. . . And now, faith, hope, and love abide; these three, and the greatest of these is love" (1 Corinthians 13:11–13). The universe matures, and does so through us, as the presence and dynamism of Love.

In the end, it comes down to telling one's own story with as much integrity as possible. Love has unceasingly made advances upon me. I know that I have been made for Love. Growing up and becoming an adult human means assuming responsibility for becoming the presence of Love, even when I fail, and when it terrifies me (which is much of the time). I know of no deeper truth in my life. It may be the height of narcissism to read my personal history back into the story of evolution, to suggest that this primal impulse that is wooing me was present from the beginning. Then again, why not start with present reality and read this back into our origins? Why not imagine that our current centre of purpose, meaning, and yearning for Love expresses an original and originating Mystery? In any case, it's my story and I'm sticking to it. It certainly seems to stick to me.

I thank the people of Canadian Memorial United Church for putting up with me for the past seventeen years. The reflections in this book were originally written as sermons delivered to them, and we have been evolving together in our understanding of what Love looks like in the context of a faith community.

I am indebted to mentors, living and dead. I've mentioned many of them in other books, so I'll just highlight a few: Dr. John Haught, whose theological writings continue to inspire; philosopher Steve McIntosh, whose careful thought acts like a compass for me; Barbara Marx Hubbard, a pioneer and a leader in the field and practice of conscious evolution; Michael Dowd and Connie Barlow, itinerate evangelists of evolution and their passionate commitment to evidence-based faith; Andrew Cohen, who is working out—at a deeper level than anybody on the planet right now—what all of this looks like in the context of a committed community; my therapist, Dr. Mia Kalef, who is, for me, the gentlest and surest of guides through the fields of Love; and American philosopher Ken Wilber, whose integral map opened up new vistas for me—this orienting map underlies many of these reflections, and I owe Ken an enormous debt of gratitude.

Most of all, I am grateful to my wife, Ann, who sees most clearly the gaps between the call to Love and how it gets played out, day by day, with one's own beloved. Ann's unceasing support for me to follow my dreams truly represents, for me, the advance of Love.

The Advance of Love

Luke 10:25-37

Ever notice that in the parable of the Good Samaritan Jesus doesn't answer the lawyer's question directly? The lawyer comes to him wanting to know what he must do to inherit eternal life. In mythic religion, this is code for: What do I have to do to get on God's good side for eternity? Jesus requires the lawyer recite the first commandment, which ends with "love your neighbour as yourself." The lawyer's job in life is to debate the fine points of religious law, so he tries to engage Jesus in a philosophical debate: Who is my neighbour? Juicy question. You could debate it till the cows come home. This is why the writer of Luke's gospel says that the lawyer was trying to "justify himself." He was trying to make himself right with God and humanity by arguing his way out of actually having to *be* a neighbour. But Jesus realizes that embedded in the question is an assumption that God only expects us to take care of our *own* people. The others, surely, we can leave by the side of the road. Jesus doesn't answer the lawyer's question.

Instead, he tells a parable and then puts a better question back to the lawyer. Who *acted* as a neighbour to the man who was beat up and robbed: the two religious men, who walked by the man in order to fulfil their religious duties, or the Samaritan, who acted with compassion, tended to the man's wounds, and generally put himself out for another person in that person's hour of need? The theological debate that the lawyer was hankering for is cut short. He is compelled to acknowledge that the man who *acted* like a neighbour was, in fact, the neighbour.

The lawyer cannot bring himself to say the words *Samaritan* and *neighbour* in the same sentence. Instead he says: "The one who showed him mercy" (10:37). In other words, the one who *acted* like a neighbour. This is Jesus's brilliance as a teacher on full display. Jews and Samaritans were enemies. Historical animosities ran deep between the two groups. Jesus forces a Jew to acknowledge that a despised Samaritan kept God's commandment while two priests of Jewish law failed to do so. As a Jew himself, we know that Jesus wasn't putting down Jews, just the Jewish priests who were so focused on religious rituals that they forgot what the spiritual life was all about. All of us know what it's like to have something "more important" to do than to care for a stranger. The lawyer is required to see and validate the Samaritan's exemplary behaviour. In so doing, the Samaritan becomes fully human to the lawyer—somebody capable of exceptional compassion. The Samaritan arises in the lawyer's consciousness, perhaps for the first time, as a model for neighbourliness.

The parable of the Good Samaritan is about empathy—in the Samaritan for the man by the side of the road, and by the end, in the lawyer for the Samaritan. It's about seeing the humanity in those whom we've been socialized to believe are less than fully human. It's about transforming the fear of difference into a realization that we're all one in our common capacity to act like neighbours. This is Jesus serving the advance of Love.

The church has a chequered history in regard to extending empathy to those who are considered to be outside of God's grace. On the one hand, the early church was radical in how it expanded its social circles of empathy to include the poor, the impure, the widowed, the outcast, children, Gentiles, and women. When these groups were invisible to the world, the church saw them and treated them as the very presence of Christ. On the other hand, when the Roman Empire appropriated Christianity as its state religion, the church lost its radical empathic edge.

After the fourth century, the church regressed. Women and children were not seen as full participants in the Kin(g)dom of God. Infidels either converted or were persecuted. Gay and lesbian people were demonized—unless they "converted" to a heterosexual lifestyle. And still today, my estimate is that 70% of the world's Christians assume that other religions are traps for unsuspecting souls. Too many Christians continue to behave like the priest and the Levite in the parable of the Good Samaritan. Religious beliefs override empathy.

This is disturbing for a precise reason: Much scientific research that is being done today shows that empathic responses are built into the very fabric of our being. It turns out that we are not as red in tooth and claw as neo-Darwinians would have us believe. We are not merely selfish, unfeeling animals, competing for our survival at any cost. Barbara King, Frans de Waal, and Elisabet Sahtouris are just a few of a growing number of scientists whose research is indicating that our evolutionary wiring includes an instinct for empathy. Brain scientists have discovered what they call "mirror neurons" in our brains. When we see another sentient being suffer, these neurons fire off in our brains, which causes us to suffer in solidarity. This is not a choice. If our brains do not get lit up by another's suffering, there is something wrong with us. We have an "empathy deficit."[1]

And here's the kicker: this response is not exclusive to humans. Hungry rats will choose starvation rather than feed themselves if they know that taking a food pellet will cause another rat to be hurt by an electric shock.[2] As it turns out, it takes a lot of brainwashing for us to override our natural empathic wiring.

---

[1] Simon Baron-Cohen, *The Science of Evil: On Empathy and the Origins of Cruelty* (New York: Basic Books, 2011), 44.

[2] Russell Church, "Emotional Reactions of Rats to the Pain of Others," *Journal of Comparative and Physiological Psychology* 52 (1959).

Ironically, mythic religion and modern scientific materialism have teamed up to get us to believe that humans are fundamentally selfish and evil. With this as the starting point, the thinking is that it takes a huge amount of training, education, and reconditioning to override our impulse to kill each other off. But in reality, it may be that massive social conditioning is required to blind us to the inherent dignity and beauty of all sentient beings. We need to be taught that Hutus or Tutsis are evil, that Jews and gypsies and homosexuals are Satan's children, that women are less worthy than men, that indigenous people are inferior, that animals don't have feelings, that those who don't accept Christ as their Lord and Saviour are condemned to hell for eternity, and that the Earth is dead and not a living system. Learning to override a natural empathic connection with all of life requires a lifetime of social conditioning—by our educational systems, religious institutions, corporate cultures, and families.

The priest and the Levite in Jesus's parable had to be taught that contact with a dead man made them unclean and that it was therefore all right to walk by the man—they would thus remain pure to perform their priestly rituals in the temple. They had to learn that God wanted them to perform religious rituals more than take care of the beaten man lying in a ditch.

Modern socialization was aided by a certain interpretation of Darwin's theory of evolution. God was sidelined. It was assumed that evolution replaced God. Dirt replaced God as the source of life. Those with a modernist worldview made a fundamental assumption about the nature of reality: namely, that the highest and most complex forms of life are the products of the lowest and simplest. They drew their conclusions about nature—including human nature—using the lowest and simplest forms of life as the interpretive key to understanding human nature. The more primitive, the more natural. Watch two hyenas competing for a carcass and conclude that this behaviour describes the core human impulse as well. Freud did the same thing with psychoanalysis, reducing civilization to the sublimated expression of our most primitive murderous and sexual impulses.

But what if we keep evolution *and* God in the picture? What if we were to reverse this modernist assumption and start with the highest expression of life we can imagine after 13.7 billion years—say a Jesus of Nazareth? What if we assumed that the intelligence, compassion, and empathy exhibited by Jesus represents the Heart of Reality? What if he is not the exception but rather a true reflection of Reality? Yes, it took human beings 200,000 years to arrive at the expression of divinity personified in a human being. But he is where the evolutionary trajectory is headed—the future, now. He defines human nature.

If Jesus is a true reflection of Reality, we can conclude that all of life emerges from the highest, most complex, and most compassionate level, which is the divine Heart. Then begins the evolutionary journey of manifesting the divine Heart within the various realms and levels of life. In the development of humanity as a species, the empathic line of intelligence evolves from just me (egocentric) to us (my tribe, my family, my nation) to all of us (the whole world) to all that is (love of the whole cosmos); the evolutionary impulse moves from egocentric to ethnocentric to worldcentric to cosmocentric. And this trajectory emerges out of, and is evolving toward, the heart of God.

In a fascinating column in the *Globe and Mail* titled "Soccer Shatters Ethnic Myths," Doug Saunders makes the point that during the 2010 Word Cup "soccer did a magical job of demolishing the lies that Europeans like to tell" about the purity of their ethnic lines. He notes that even while Germans wrapped themselves in the national flag during the World Cup, the ethnic background of the star players they revered so deeply was diverse. For example, the grandfather of their star midfielder, Mesut Özil, is one of two million Germans born in Turkey. Jérôme Boateng's dad is from Ghana; Cacau is a black, Brazilian German, and Nuremberg supporters love him. On down the roster, Saunders goes. The last names of no fewer than eleven

German players are decidedly not Teutonic. He then goes on to quote researchers who found that the ethnic mixing of the players for England and France did more to overcome racism in those countries than anything else. People couldn't hide their fervent love for their superstar players, despite their ethnic backgrounds, which has translated into measurable sociological changes.

We have undergone a virtual explosion of the empathic impulse since the 1960s. If you don't believe it, watch a series like *Mad Men* to get a glimpse of the sexist attitudes of men and the invisibility of women in the early 1960s. At the same time as we are destroying our planet—the result of the Industrial Revolution and the indignities of the modernist worldview—another worldview is in the process of emerging. The postmodernist worldview is emerging out of an awareness of some of the shortcomings of modernism. The particular line of intelligence that has been awakened in the last fifty years is empathy. We allowed ourselves to show our sensitivity as a species, our essential neighbourliness. We recognized that we have a heart.

Everybody and everything is now a neighbour. After ten thousand years of active suppression, women's equality became obvious; Martin Luther King Jr., Nelson Mandela, Malcolm X, and others raised up the rights of black people and shamed the assumption of white male privilege; this past winter, I watched a sledge hockey game played by men who had lost at least one limb—the venue was sold out; we can no longer hit children without being shamed by society; I have presided in our sanctuary at the celebration of maybe a dozen gay marriages.

In his groundbreaking book, *The Empathic Civilization*, Jeremy Rifkin tracks the evidence for social evolution from the dawn of civilization and notes that former boundaries separating people of diverse backgrounds are starting to fall. For example, Rifkin's research states that among Jews over the age of fifty-five, only 20% of married people have non-Jewish spouses. Among Jews between thirty-five and fifty-four, 37% have non-Jewish spouses, and for those under thirty-five, the percentage of those with non-Jewish spouses has reached 41%; the same trend exists between Protestants, Catholics, and Muslims.

Rifkin offers Germany as a dramatic example of the trends in marriage patterns. In 1960, nearly every marriage was between Germans. (Only one in twenty-five involved a foreign-born national.) By 1994, one of every seven partners in marriage was foreign born.

In 1958, two black boys in North Carolina, aged seven and nine, were arrested, convicted, and sentenced to twelve to fourteen years in prison after a white girl had kissed them. According to Rifkin's research, by 1987, only 48% of Americans agreed with the statement "I think it's all right for blacks and whites to date each other," and 25% said they had little in common with people of other races. By 2003, 77% of people said it's all right for blacks and whites to date each other. What about interracial marriage? In 1958, only 4% of whites approved of intermarriage with blacks. By 1997, 67% of whites approved of intermarriage between blacks and whites. And for those born after 1976, the issue of skin colour virtually becomes a non-issue.

Our empathic impulse is beginning to encompass nonhuman species. In 2008, Ecuador legislated that nonhuman species and ecosystems have the legal right to thrive.[3]

We live in an age when the leading edge of Spirit is manifesting as the impulse to see the other as a neighbour and to not allow artificial differences to block our natural empathic impulses. Christ breaks down the walls that separate us, at the artificial boundaries we have constructed to justify our beliefs, prejudices, and false divisions that cause us to walk right by suffering and refuse to respond. Christ is the Heart of the evolutionary impulse that interrupts our carefully mapped-out agendas and calls us to follow our own hearts to the other side of the road to do what we knew to be natural and right before we were taught otherwise.

---

[3] See *The Empathic Civilization* by Jeremy Rifkin (New York: Penguin Group Inc., 2009), pages 425 to 475, for a comprehensive summary of these empathic trends.

Nothing and Nobody Against Us

Genesis 32:22-31

I'm interested in the "nothing and nobody is against us" principle of living[1] because most of us expend a whole lot of energy complaining (I was going to say, "whining," but that seemed uncharitable), which comes from an unconscious assumption that life is aligned against us. We can end up feeling like victims in a vast, uncaring universe. Or worse, that the universe is actually aligned against us.

Andrew Cohen is the guru of a community that takes conscious evolution seriously. He writes and speaks with the lucidity of one who knows the terrain intimately, and in his new book, *Evolutionary Enlightenment*, he challenges his readers to clarify their assumptions about the fundamental nature of life. For example, he asks: How do we make sense of the big bang? A universe came roaring into existence, starting out as an unimaginably dense point of matter and energy, and it turned into us after thousands of millions of years. Andrew asks, "When something came from nothing was it a big Yes, a big No, or a big Neutral?" How we answer that will determine whether we feel as though the universe is for us, against us, or whether it couldn't care less about us.

What if we unconsciously assume that the big bang is a big "no"? Some religious systems have thought so. They tell us that this universe

[1] Gary Simmons, *The I of the Storm: Embracing Conflict, Creating Peace* (Wellington: Unity Books, 2001).

9

is an illusion; to exist is to suffer, and the goal of the religious life should be to escape suffering. Some ancient Gnostics sects (certainly not the majority) believed that the world was the result of a subordinate god—a demiurge—and that our journey was to wake up and escape the world. Christian theology that assumes that heaven is a better place to be than Earth, and that getting there is the goal of this life, is based in this assumption. The various "rapture" scenarios of some Christian sects portray people flying off the planet, toward heaven, to receive their reward. When you believe that the event that brought all of this into existence is a big no, then spiritual practice is all about transcending, that is, exiting, this world for some better existence somewhere else—whether it be a blissed-out state of consciousness or heaven.

Or was the big bang a big "neutral"? This sounds a little strange, but it is actually the modernist worldview, in which life is a cosmic accident. For modernists, this accident represents the random collision of atoms that were sparked into life by chemical interactions and electricity, and the universe has no intrinsic meaning and purpose except that which we choose to give it. But, they believe, those meanings are arbitrary constructions of a meaning-making creature who accidentally became conscious and couldn't abide a meaningless existence. So the conscious creature made up stories as a defence against purposelessness. Today, it is considered very sophisticated and intelligent to think like this. The really smart people know that it's all a ruse: religion was all right for our early ancestors because *they* didn't know any better. But now we have science and reason. "Reasonable" people know that religion is merely an opiate or a crutch, that when you grow up, you can live without these kinds of props, without stories that try to make meaning out of an amoral, directionless existence.

Or was the big bang a big "yes"? This would mean that life is essentially good. It has purpose. It's going somewhere. All emergent forms, from cells to centipedes to conscious humans, are ecstatic creations of a primordial Mind and Heart that said yes to life, a universe flashed into existence in response to this ecstatic, urgent yes. While we may not be able to figure out the big picture in all its details, there *is* a big picture, and we're a part of it. We are the conscious part of evolution that is able to see patterns of meaning and purpose everywhere. Everything is a manifestation of that original yes to the great emergence of life. We ourselves become a glimpse of where it's all headed. We notice our creativity, our capacity for choice, the love in our hearts, our capacity to suffer with others who are in pain, and the ecstatic joy of being alive, and we conclude that whatever Mind it was that said the yes to life was *for* us. But even more significantly, we begin to imagine, as the mystics we are, that we are that Mind evolving. Our yes to being alive is the same yes that gave birth to a universe.

And getting this matter straight becomes really important when life is hard, when it's not going as we think it should, when life feels like a wrestling match. This brings me to one of the most colourful stories in the Bible, the story of Jacob. Where the story picks up at Genesis 32:22, Jacob's past has finally caught up with him.

A couple of decades earlier, Jacob had tricked his brother out of his birthright inheritance, and then he took off for Uncle Laban's farm—mostly for protection from his outraged brother, Esau. Now, on the banks of the river Jabbok, it's time for Jacob's reckoning with Consequence. Jacob sent all his family, his livestock, and all his wealth ahead. He is alone, not knowing whether his brother will welcome him or murder him when the sun rises. It is a dark night of the soul.

In this wonderful legend, a man whose identity is somewhat ambiguous comes to Jacob. Is it an angel or is it God? Is it his past that has finally caught up with him? Or is this strange figure all of these rolled into this singular moment of reckoning? Jacob is about to be in the wrestling match of his life, and the outcome is by no means guaranteed.

It's at these moments that it's critical how we have answered the question of the ultimate nature of life: Is it a yes, a no, or is it meaningless? When we're having a bad day, or when we're challenged by circumstances that are very difficult (an illness, an unexpected death, a dissatisfied partner), we will interpret the ensuing period of struggle, the meaning of our suffering, according to our fundamental assumption about the nature of life itself.

If we believe that the universe is a big no, then when life gets tough, we'll try to escape. We'll escape into meditation, hedonism, alcohol or drugs, television, work, or shopping. Our assumption that life is against us will result in a life of denial. We won't face the challenges life throws our way because we believe they've come to destroy us. Life is overpowering. It's all too much for us, and we didn't ask for any of this anyway. We will become victims of circumstance when fate catches up to us. Our mantras will be, "It's not fair," and, "What did I do to deserve this?" Our suffering will confirm our assumption that life is against us.

Let's change the unconscious assumption. If our answer is that life is a big neutral, a random accident, then we're likely to say to ourselves, "Well, why *not* me? It's all a crapshoot anyway, and circumstances just caught up with me. There is no meaning to what has happened to me. At best, I may stoically face 'reality.'" If we believe this, we are not so much victims as we are flashes of life, quantum particles that popped into existence out of the cosmic vacuum, and we shall eventually return to that realm. If our challenger is an unwelcome illness, we will heroically fight it—fight for a few more years on this island of rock hurtling nowhere in particular through space and signifying nothing. But the illness will not be our teacher: it has no wisdom to offer us. It is what it is, nothing more. Our suffering will confirm our nihilistic assumptions about a meaningless existence. The required virtue for the journey is courage, and the best we can do is to remain courageous in the face of a vast, indifferent universe.

But if the fundamental nature of life is good, if it is a big yes, if it is imbued with meaning, purpose, and significance from the get-go, we will become curious about our suffering. We will assume that challenges and challengers have come to be our teachers. The universe is a living, learning organism, come to conscious awareness in us, and so our suffering holds the promise of wisdom. If we are truly committed to go twelve rounds with those challenges, to face everything that comes our way—even if takes every last drop of energy we have—we will reap a harvest of spiritual growth.

We will assume, in fact, that God is *in* the challenges—even when it feels like a confrontation, as it did for Jacob. A deep curiosity will arise, and we will ask, "Why now? What can I learn? How is this shaping me and providing me with the resources to fulfil my destiny?" No, it won't mean an end to suffering. And, ultimately, nobody is getting out of here alive. But even death, we will discover, is in the service of life, and our own lives, no matter how long or short, are a process of great significance. We will know that our whole lives have been an expression of the universe's yes to being—alive, awake, and engaged. It's all a great spiritual adventure, and how we engage the adventure has ultimate significance because we sense that a future wants to emerge through us that nobody else can quite accomplish. As Paul wrote in his letter to the Romans: "If God is for us, who is against us?" (Romans 8:31).

A caveat: not all suffering is purposeful, sent by God to teach us a lesson. In the Norwegian case of the Oslo bombing and shootings at a youth camp, both caused by a psychopathic killer in the summer of 2011, all that's left to do in response to such a tragedy is to grieve. But if we've come to a place of trusting that the nature of life itself is a yes, then we will interpret the events as actions of someone who is deeply misaligned with Reality as opposed to interpreting the tragedy as proof that life sucks. We will be more likely, in the wake of this kind of senseless suffering, to assume that God will also be with us in our grief and in our struggle to engage with life again.

Getting to yes doesn't solve life's problems. Rather, we will see our problems as evolutionary provocations to help us deepen and grow in intimacy with a living universe. We will almost certainly receive a wound, as Jacob did, leaving his wrestling match with a limp. But it will be an exquisite wound, representing our willingness to engage with blood, sweat, tears, and great joy. We will have become spiritual warriors.

Jacob receives a name change. He is no longer Jacob, a name that symbolized all of the personal, familial, and cultural constructions that we try to squeeze ourselves into, like a coat that no longer fits. His name is Israel, which means "one who has striven with God and prevailed." This coat fits his expanded identity, his authentic self. Israel is no longer running from God, from his past, or from his radiant future. He has arrived at a place in life where he is going to face everything, because everything, and every experience, is a portal into the Mind and Heart of the divine once you are committed unambiguously, unhesitatingly to life.

Please don't assume that just because you are warm and vertical, or because you are successful, or because you have what culture calls a good life that you have uttered this primal yes. Only you, in the depths of your soul, know if you are all in or if you are hedging your bets.

The biblical witness is that we are in a covenant relationship with the God of life, with the One who uttered that first, primal, "Yes, let it be and let it all become." The promise of that God is that after our dark nights of the soul, Love awaits us, as it awaited Jacob. We may need a crutch, or a sibling's strong shoulder to lean on, but Love will lead us, limping, into our next adventure.

The Mystery of Growth

2 Corinthians 5:16–17, Mark 4:26–28

Paul was all about discerning what aspects of his religion needed to be left behind and what he needed carry forward. This discernment even extended to his name. Saul was a really, really smart rabbi who didn't appreciate an upstart peasant rabbi like Jesus of Nazareth upsetting the theological apple cart with his new-fangled teaching. So, when the religious authorities needed a volunteer to round up the followers of this new spirituality and put an end to the fledgling movement, Saul volunteered.

But Saul was so shattered by his encounter with the risen Jesus that by the time a couple of disciples picked him up off the road to Damascus and dusted him off, he had undergone an identity shift. He needed a new name. He became, to use his own phrase, "a new creation" in Christ (2 Corinthians 5:17). Saul became Paul.

Because Paul was so smart, he did an interesting thing with all the teachings of Jesus that he received from the other apostles. He never, ever talked about them in his letters. It's not that he didn't know the parables of Jesus. It's that somebody else was doing Jesus's teachings. It was in hand. But he had a distinct contribution to make. He took the teachings of Jesus and transformed them into teachings *about* Jesus. Just as Paul's name evolved, Paul's calling was to take this movement to a new level. This is what he's getting at when he writes:

> From now on, therefore, we regard no one from a human point
> of view; even though we once knew Christ from a human point
> of view, we know him no longer in that way. (2 Corinthians 5:16)

In other words, Jesus's body was barely cold, the disciples were just trying to figure out how to pass on Jesus's teachings to the world, a crucial element to ensure the survival of the movement, and Paul was saying: "Yeah, but you know what, Peter and James and John, you're missing a piece by focusing only on Jesus's teachings. . . Let's start thinking about his big identity. Let's start thinking about the *cosmic* dimensions of what God was doing in Jesus." Paul started thinking *about* Jesus as the embodiment of sacred Wisdom—the same Wisdom (Sophia in the First Testament) out of which a universe was born. He started imagining that God was reconciling all of creation to God-self in and through Jesus's life, death, and resurrection. Paul began to think that a new age had been ushered in. A "new creation" had begun, and if you wanted proof, you didn't need to look any farther than Paul's own transformed life.

Very early in his life as a follower of Christ, Paul was already an active agent in the evolution of the Jesus tradition. Paul's intentional evolution of the tradition is Spirit-led, and, therefore, the church is called to re-enact this evolutionary impulse in every generation. In doing so, Paul was enacting the same impulse that was in Jesus, who began many of his teachings with the phrase, "You have heard it said, but I say unto you. . ." This is the core of what it means to be church. We receive with gratitude the tradition of our ancestors, and we allow the tradition to evolve through us. This is what it means to be "in Christ."

The apostles in Jerusalem really didn't know what to do with Paul. He was pushing them to the edge of their identity as Jews. He was crossing boundaries, perhaps even transgressing boundaries: the Gentiles were welcome; they didn't have to eat kosher food or get circumcised; they didn't have to observe Jewish rituals. For Paul, God had done something radically new in Jesus of Nazareth, and the disciples weren't getting it.

Paul writes: "if anyone is in Christ, there is a new creation: everything old has passed away; see, everything has become new!" (5:17)

Jesus tells a story about a seed, one of his favourite images. He says that the Kin(g)dom of God is like a seed that a farmer scatters. After a few nights of sleep, the farmer arises one morning, and, sure enough, the seed has sprouted. But the farmer doesn't have a clue how it happened. He just knows that it's going to put food on the table for his family. Now, if you are a subsistence farmer, you're likely to give this whole mystery only passing consideration. You've got work to do. You don't have a lot of time to ponder the mystery of growth. But if you are a follower of Jesus, he's going to plop you down in front of a wheat field and require that you consider it deeply. Because, if you get this piece, you get the Kin(g)dom of God, and if you get the Kin(g)dom of God from the inside out, you get what Jesus is on about.

In Mark 4:26–28 Jesus invites his followers to look at the mystery of growth. He wants them to suspend ordinary functional consciousness ("Seeds just grow and then we harvest the seeds and make bread and eat it, so that's a good thing") and look at the process—the dynamics of growth. "Earth," says Jesus, "produces of itself." That's the key line in the whole parable. Earth is a living organism within a living universe that knows how to do life. This wisdom comes as standard equipment in creation. Life emerges. Scientists have names for it: self-organization, autopoiesis, and emergence. But these are just fancy words that describe the religious sensibility that anybody who has spent any time at all pondering the meaning of life feels—Mystery. And "mystery" is not the sum total of what we do not know but might know one day when science gets around to figuring it out. This is not a detective novel and it's not something that will ever be solved. Mystery is about entering into the interior depths of Reality, there to be apprehended by the One, the Oneness, the Source of all this life, the Spirit from whom all creation emerges. The religious life is about falling back in love with life, with the Mystery of all it all, with the One in whom this life emerges.

There is implicit evolutionary awareness in the way the parable is told—first the seed, then the sprout, then the stalk, then the flower, and then the harvesting. It's obvious that there is developmental growth. But I believe that Jesus was attempting to make his disciples aware that this developmental growth happens *in them* as well. The same Spirit from which the seed grows into a fully mature plant is animating them, growing them, and awakening them to their full potential. In fact, if you spend much time pondering the mystery of evolutionary development, you come to a mystical awareness that *we* are the seeds, and that the same mysterious power that we observe animating a plant also animates our growth. We're meant to come to full flower. Before the end of our life, all that we have done, all that we have been, all that we have contributed will be harvested to serve the ongoing evolutionary journey of the cosmos.

If Earth produces of itself, then the same must be true for us. After all, we are the presence of Earth in human form. We are the fruit of the Great Emergence. What else can we be? Give Earth 4.5 billion years, leave it to "produce of itself," and the planet produces human beings, with bodies and minds, with flesh and spirit, with instincts and conscious awareness. This is both spiritual mystery and good science. Therefore we also "produce of ourselves." We are, each of us, a medium of sacred, creative Mystery. And this surely describes the history of the human species. From the start, we have been creating new modes of human presence. New and more complex levels of consciousness, new forms of governing ourselves, and new technologies have all emerged—not always for the best and not always in accordance with sacred Wisdom. Yet, we are undeniably centres of creative emergence. An evolutionary, sacred intelligence is coursing through you and through me. And when we open to this intelligence, it begins to dawn on us that we are not separate from the processes that created us. We *are* that process in human form. To know this is to access the creative power of a universe. To own it is to receive a new, expanded identity. This empirically based condition of unity with all that is, is why I call this way of imaging life in Christ evolutionary Christian mysticism.

While visiting Florence, Italy, my wife and I visited the Gallery of the Accademia di Belle Arti, where Michelangelo's *David* is on display. I can only imagine that when Michelangelo was working, he became one with the creative intelligence of the universe. *David* is an astonishing feat of creativity. But the sculptures that had the greatest impact on us were the *Prisoners*. These are the statues of human figures that he didn't finish. They're trapped in the marble, prisoners in stone, struggling to be free and whole. They capture the inner yearning of humans to be released into our fullness and our freedom of being. The difference between those imprisoned marble figures and us, however, is that we can consciously cooperate in our own release. We can chip away at whatever it is that confines us. It's a lifelong project. And if we get free enough, we can even dedicate ourselves to helping others to gain their freedom.

This creative project of growing into fullness and freedom is the prime directive of the universe. It's another built-in feature of the universe—a God force, if you like. Our little self doesn't generate it. This is a soul-sized project. It's what is behind the mystery of growth and evolution. It is the call of the Christ.

By declaring that we intend to "teach and practise evolutionary Christian mysticism," the congregation I serve is saying that we are willing to enter what Jesus called the Kin(g)dom of God and allow ourselves to explore as fully as possible the mystery of growth: that we are seeds of God; that we are the medium, the earth that produces of itself; that we are farmers who reap this harvest of creative potential, and, finally, when you get to the bottom of it all, we are embodied forms of the mystery of a sacred evolutionary impulse. All of this is what it means to be in Christ—the old has passed away and every-thing has become new!

What does this mean for congregations? Like the farmer, we'll have to wait and see. I do know that we will not strive to engineer our future into existence but rather to trust the emergent impulse of the universe. We won't try to be clever and force life into existence. There's no need. We'll hold our five-year strategies lightly. Rather, we'll create habitats for growth in our worship, our educational programs, our way of being together in the community, and in the way we govern ourselves. We will embrace a natural design as much as possible. We don't claim to know *how* the growth happens any more than a farmer knows how the seed grows. But we will know that it's a sign of Spirit in our midst. We will continue to help people discover their gifts for ministry and then release them into their calling, and we will call the garden that emerges "church." It will be more like an English garden, I suspect, than a French one (French gardens convey, to me, a need to impose the modernist impulse to control nature). We will tend this garden, as all gardens must be tended in order to flourish, and there will be those who love to deadhead and prune, and those who love to pick the flowers and make beautiful arrangements; there will be those who haul in the manure and those who are always dreaming up new garden beds.

We will tap into an evolutionary intelligence that is on the as-cent right now on our planet, that our tradition calls Sophia or sa-cred Wisdom, and claims was incarnate in Jesus of Nazareth. And this much we know: it will continue to be a great adventure, discovering One who makes all things new.

Kicking the Apocaholic Habit

Luke 24:13–32

The Rational Optimist by Dr. Matt Ridley is a book that rubs the post-modernist pessimist the wrong way, and it threw me for a loop. The guy is an unapologetic optimist. But what's really infuriating is that he's got an evidence-based optimism. He actually has numbers and hard data to back up his claim that the world has been getting better for a long time, and there's no reason to think the trend won't continue.

I fussed and fumed my way through the book, putting it down every fifteen minutes, trying to convince myself that this guy is an intellectual lightweight. (Actually, he's a heavyweight.)[1] Or that he is a greedy capitalist wearing rose-coloured glasses. (He is a believer in a free market, and the exchange of goods and services, but not financial products. And, yes, he has been implicated in the Northern Rock banking crisis in Britain).[2] My radar was up for any unsubstantiated claim, any misinterpretation of the facts, any possible slip-up that would reinforce my pessimism. Allow me to share a rather lengthy excerpt from chapter 1 just to give you a sense of how infuriating this guy can be.

---

[1] Ridley is a doctor of philosophy (in zoology) and former editor of *The Economist*. His books include *The Origins of Virtue* and *Genome*. See rationaloptimist.com/cv for a rundown of his top credentials.

[2] For a scathing critique of Matt Ridley's work, read "Matt Ridley's Rational Optimist is Telling the Rich What They Want to Hear," by George Monbiot at guardian.co.uk.

Ridley compares 2005 with 1955:

[In 2005, the] average human being on Planet Earth earned nearly three times as much money (corrected for inflation), ate one-third more calories of food, buried one-third as many of her children and could expect to live one-third longer. She was less likely to die as a result of war, murder, childbirth, accidents, tornadoes, flooding, famine, whooping cough, tuberculosis, malaria, diphtheria, typhus, typhoid, measles, smallpox, scurvy or polio. She was less likely, at any given age, to get cancer, heart disease or stroke. She was more likely to be literate and to have finished school. She was more likely to own a telephone, a flush toilet, a refrigerator and a bicycle. All this during a half-century when the world population has more than doubled, so that far from being rationed by population pressure, the goods and services available to the people of the world have expanded. It is, by any standard, an astonishing human achievement.[3]

I could go on. But you get the idea. Arguing statistics is a mug's game, and there are dangers with using percentages, admittedly. I'm not saying that I've had the time to integrate or check all of his facts. But what really interests me is that when I come across statistics in support of apocalyptic scenarios, I rarely feel the need to check them in the same way. What's that about? Some part of me just accepts, as a default position, that the world is getting a lot worse, that we've reached a turning point, that the end is near, and that human beings are hopeless.

Although, within the last year I received an email that caused me so much despair that I thought I had better check out the facts for myself. You may remember it: The email had photos of evil Costa Ricans who were gathering up baby sea turtles from the beach. The turtles are a delicacy in that country and have been for hundreds of years. They are also endangered, and here was photographic proof that the human species cared more about their stomachs than Earth's creatures. How could we be so cruel and short-sighted? Well, as it turned

---

[3] Matt Ridley, *The Rational Optimist: How Prosperity Evolves* (New York: HarperCollins Publishers, 2010), 14.

out, the photo was of a legal sea-turtle harvest. On this single beach, for a three-day period, once a year, the people are allowed to gather the turtles. It's illegal all year round at all other beaches. It was a compromise that has been very successful in dramatically reducing poaching and the black market for sea turtles. The sea turtle population in this area is increasing, not decreasing. By the time I uncovered the real story of the photo, I had received at least ten despairing emails from friends. Good news had actually been turned into bad news.

Halfway through the book, Ridley used a term that was coined by Gary Alexander to describe people like me: *apocaholics!* I'm addicted to apocalyptic scenarios. You know that you may need to go into a twelve-step program if you walk into a bookstore and the only ones that attract you are the ones that tell you that it's already too late for the human species; any title with the phrase *turning point* causes you to twitch uncontrollably—as in, "the human species is at a turning point." Ridley calls this "turning-pointitis," infuriatingly documenting the multiple occasions over the past fifty years when various writers have solemnly warned that we were at a turning point. Each came and went.

Walk through any airport bookstore and check out the current-affairs section. All my favourite apocalyptic prophets are there: Noam Chomsky, Barbara Ehrenreich, Al Gore, John Gray, Naomi Klein, George Monbiot, Michael Moore. Ridley makes the point that all these good people, in one way or another, come to the same conclusions: (1) the world is a terrible place, (2) it's getting worse, (3) it's mostly the fault of commerce, and (4) a turning point has been reached. I respect each of these writers. They serve us well in pointing out the indignities of the modernist mindset and agenda. But, I have to confess, that rarely, if ever, do any of them mention any of the dignities. But, like any addict, I can't stay away from them. I should try heroin. At least (I'm told) you feel good for a little while after the fix.

I'm not alone. In the evolution of worldviews, postmodernism emerged, in part, as a reaction against the indignities of the modernist/

achievist worldview. This was an important cultural evolution. It helped us to take a clear look at all of those who were left behind by the modernist agenda. The modernists' exclusive focus on progress and economic growth seemed to lack a heart. Postmodernist pessimism serves to balance the overly optimistic worldview of modernism. But postmodernist sensitivity has its own ideological blind spot. Just try telling somebody who sees the world through this lens that the world is getting better!

What's after postmodernism? Is there no good news? Is there really no hope? Is it realistic to imagine that we can deconstruct the entire free-market system, and return to agrarian or tribal self-sufficiency, as many environmentalists imagine? Could we collectively imagine what Paul Hawkens, Amory Lovins, and L. Hunter Lovins call "natural capitalism,"[4] a free-market system that mimics Earth's processes? Can we admit that modernism has actually provided the species with a deep sense of our human potential, and capacity for innovation and adaptation? Is it possible that economic development will help Africa, not massive financial-aid programs, which are clearly not working? And when somebody like Ridley points out that the only way Africa is going to emerge and join the rest of the world is to use chemical fertilizers and fossil fuels, and this will save lives and save habitats (greater productivity equals less land needed to grow food, equals more habitat for nonhuman species), what stops us from at least listening? I know the case against chemical fertilizers very well, but why have I never seriously considered the case *for* them? Whatever comes next will need to be based in pragmatic idealism, with an equal focus on pragmatism and idealism.

There are, indeed, very serious challenges facing us as a species. Our way of being on the planet is imperilling other life forms. But it would help us look these challenges clearly in the face if we did so

---

[4] Paul Hawken, Amory B. Lovins, and L. Hunter Lovins, *Natural Capitalism: The Next Industrial Revolution* (Washington, DC: Earthscan LLC, 2010).

with the narrative of resiliency and evolutionary adaptation as the context for the narratives of despair. What every apocalyptic scenario has underestimated for the past two hundred years is the truly amazing capacity of human beings to adapt and thrive, as well as the resiliency of Earth. What is rarely taken into account is how our collective intelligence is growing exponentially, that we are able to adapt with ever-increasing speed. And that Earth is amazing in Her self-renewing, self-organizing, self-regulating capacity. Up to this point, we have found a way through the various crises. Why can't we believe that the same will be true of our time?

In 1830, Thomas Babington Macaulay put this question to the apocaholics of his day: "On what principle is it, that when we see nothing but improvement behind us, we are to expect nothing but deterioration before us?"[5]

The disciples are walking home on the road to Emmaus. They are devastated. All their hope resided in Jesus and he was executed. They have good reason to despair. They had hoped, the story says, that "he was the one" (Luke 24:21). But the stranger they meet isn't interested in their hopelessness. He walks up to them and asks them what they are talking about. They share with him their discourse of despair. And then he interrupts their discourse with a narrative of hope. He's not denying reality. (Remember, in this story, the risen Christ is the same guy who was *crucified*.) But he's about to set this story within a larger story of hope. All these things that happened, he tells them, were "necessary." They were necessary, not in the fatalistic sense of being predetermined, but rather, they were preparatory. All these things were a precondition for the emergence of a new humanity and a new hope. To the narrative of "all these things that *had* happened," another chapter would be added. It would tell the story of the all the things that *could* happen in response.

---

[5] Thomas Babingon Macaulay, *Critical and Historical Essays Contributed to "The Edinburgh Review"* (London: Longman, Brown, Greens, and Longmans, 1850), 120.

And that story is grounded in the creative power of the divine Heart that is always and everywhere, in every day and age, moving in creation to fashion the best world possible. This creative power is always and forever rising up in those who have stepped inside this story of hope and made it their own, of those who have committed not merely to *proclaim* the story of hope but to *show up* as the very presence of hope in a world addicted to despair. To follow Christ is to interrupt discourses of despair as a spiritual practice. It is to allow an alternative story to shape us.

After the stranger fed the disciples' bodies with bread and fish, and their souls with hope, he left them. But he left them with hearts of fire. "Did not our hearts burn within us as he spoke"? They burned with the fire of expectancy. Death and despair had lost dominion over their lives because they had been nourished by the Heart and Creativity and Love from which the whole cosmos emerged. So rise up. Allow yourself to burn with hope. I'm pretty sure the world won't come to an end.

No Way Around Herod

Matthew 2:1-12

To get to the stable, we have to contend with Herod—the part of us that resists and subverts realizing our spiritual depths. The story of the Magi's meeting with Herod is an important part of the Christmas story, but it's not historical fact. It is a creation of the author of Matthew's gospel. The writer took the story of the pharaoh's order to execute all male Hebrew children from Exodus and brilliantly adapted it for the story of Jesus's birth.

And, despite not being historical fact, it conveys psychological and spiritual truth. There is a part of our personality that is constellated around an emotion so deep and pervasive that it acts to sabotage any idea, belief, behaviour, attitude, or person that threatens its existence. That emotion is fear. The feeling of fear is connected with our early instinctual self, which is correlated to the reptilian and neo-mammalian parts of our brain. The drive for sustenance, security, sex, and status is a natural part of all of us. But when these drives predominate, you end up with a Herod on your hands.

The word we often use for this fear-dominated self is *ego*. But when Freud coined the term *ego*, he simply meant the "I"—the part of us that we think of when we think of "me." This I mediates between the superego, which is like our inner grown-up, and the id—or the "it," all those unconscious impulses, which, until we bring them into consciousness, rule us from below. The ego is the self-organizing system that does the best it can to fashion our internal vortex of energies into a coherent, functional self—a minor miracle. A healthy ego is a gift, and much of life is about learning to be civil and hold down a job—and the capacity to do minimal damage in relationships and maybe even give a little back. Seriously, if the human race could advance this far, it would be nirvana. Let's say we're able to pull this off; we would have accomplished the fashioning of a healthy *psychological* self-system.

But sometimes this self-system gets stuck, and it is usually because of fear born of trauma. Under stress, our "I" will always regress to points in life when fear caused it to stop evolving. This is a defensive gesture. But the defence is so fierce that the mechanisms and processes we put in place to protect ourselves restrict the spontaneous expression of life within us. Freedom to act in the world is restricted by avoiding any situation, thought, or person that might trigger the fear.

An alternative strategy of avoidance is to attack. Enter Herod. Herod is the survivor within each one of us. This part of us is constantly scanning the horizon for potential threats and preparing to defend the kingdom of the little self. Herod is the unhealthy part of our self-system that does not want us to make it to the cradle of Christ-consciousness for fear of being usurped. When a power that transcends (yet includes) the ego threatens to take the throne, the Herod within us obstructs transformation. He is great at defending a kingdom (of the self) when survival is at stake, but he does not know when to stand down in the face of a higher power.

In the Christmas story, the Magi report to Herod that there is one born who is said to be king of the Jews. Well, if you happen to be the reigning king, that's a pretty big trigger. Herod begins his elaborate scheme. The best way to sabotage the Magi's spiritual journey is to destroy what they are seeking. We should not underestimate the ruthless nature of our fear-based self. It will stop at nothing to "defend" us from perceived threats.

The Magi represent the part of us that desires to organize our lives around a higher spiritual consciousness—Christ consciousness. Think of the journey the Magi took to get to Bethlehem. We're going to need that same sacred impulse, that unswerving intention of the soul, if we are to make it there. Herod has other plans. He issues a death order.

Proverbs 1:7 tells us that "the fear of God is the beginning of wisdom." We have learned to reinterpret "fear" as "awe" in order to get away from the traditional associations with a punishing God. But if we said instead, "*Understanding* our fear of God (or fear of anything) is the beginning of wisdom," we'd have the foundation for a spiritual practice that could liberate us. Our inner Herod, you see, is not crazy. He or she is merely acting in our defence, or in the gospel story, in the defence of Caesar's kingdom. He believes that the birth of this Christ child is genuinely a threat to the throne. Likewise, my inner Herod is doing its best to make sure that I don't get hurt, embarrassed, or shamed. It doesn't want me to be put in a position where I might be seen as a fraud, or fail at a calling that is beyond my ego's capacity. So, we need to surface our deepest fears and squarely face how our defence system is keeping us from growing. We need to deal with Herod, not as an evil enemy, but as a frightened defender of the kingdom of the little self.

The Magi symbolize the presence of sacred Wisdom within. This part of us is savvy about Herod's intentions. Our inner Magi understand Herod's fears but refuse to be taken in by his various schemes, which are legion and ingenious. Once you practise the awareness of fear, you realize that our wounded ego is very resourceful and very resilient. Through this practice of bringing our Magi to bear on our fears over time, those fears will certainly dissipate, but they will never disappear.

Sometimes, we just need to outsmart Herod—which is what the Magi in the story do. They listen to him, but they do not obey. They bring the drama to consciousness, but they are not swayed. They are asked to send word to Caesar the moment they find the child. Of course, they do not follow orders, knowing that Caesar is like a jealous older sibling who is not at all thrilled when the new baby arrives on the scene.

Our inner Magi invite us to go beyond our psychological or personal self. To actually realize a healthy self is an astounding accomplishment, but there is another dimension that transcends, yet includes, this self. Some call this the "Unique self."[1] Others call it the "authentic Self."[2] Still others call it the soul. Whatever you call it, it emerges from an impulse to transcend all the dramas and dreams of the personal self by tapping into a more universal or cosmic self. This is the part of us that knows our lives are for the advancement of Love.

This transpersonal self knows and honours one's own personal narrative, and all that has gone into this story. The story is never lost. It is simply contextualized. You start to identify more with the Spirit-infused evolutionary impulse of the universe. Projects focused on personal success and status become less motivating. It's not that early instinctual urges disappear. You just learn to accept and enjoy these instincts, and then get on with getting to the stable.

This is my vision for congregations: to create an evolutionary culture in which people can learn to go beyond fear-based personalities and to increasingly identify with the soul—our Christ self. Think of the soul as the deepest aspect of our identity before it becomes totally identified with Spirit. It forms a bridge between the little self and Spirit. As you move into this transpersonal realm, two things happen simultaneously. At the level of the individual, your *unique* identity begins to emerge. This is your unique, creative expression and contribution that God or the universe needs from you, the "you" who stands trembling at the evolutionary edge where Spirit has led you. You discover your deep

---

[1] Rabbi Dr. Marc Gafni.

[2] Andrew Cohen and the EnlightenNext community.

joy. At the same time, your sense of self becomes, paradoxically, more collective. The membrane between you and other people, creatures, plants, stars becomes more permeable as you experience yourself as one part of a much larger whole. You are the part that manifests the whole—a perfect representation of all that is, gathered up in you. This unity of your most creative, unique self and your identification with the whole of reality is your soul.

It can be an exacting journey to get even a glimpse of your soul. You must be able to witness your basic fears and survival instincts without identifying with them. First, you must realize a coherent, psychological self-sense. And then you will realize that you are actually bigger, much bigger, than your personal, psychological self. When you come to this realization, you begin the journey to Bethlehem. And when you are really serious about it, then you will have to deal with Herod. Your soul has a singular focus: to get to Bethlehem and pay homage to the sacred child. Your soul wants to fly to God, but Herod thinks your gifts were meant for him. There is no way to the stable except through Herod.

You will dream bigger, and a voice will sound: "Who do you think you are?"

You will lose interest in personal dramas that once were a deep source of fascination and expended energy, and a voice will sound: "You are nobody without these dramas and narratives. Cling to them for dear life. Create the conditions in your life to re-enact the drama."

You will decide to begin a regular spiritual practice, and the distractions and excuses for not starting will gather in number and in urgency.

You will take action, and then be confronted by roadblocks and setbacks.

You will be filled with conviction, and then, in the middle of the night, you will be filled with doubts. Your project will seem hopeless; your dreams, grandiose; your strategy, ill conceived. Maybe the whole journey has been an illusion.

"Fear not," the angels said to the shepherds, to Mary, to Joseph, to the Magi, and to practically anybody who got involved in any way with Jesus of Nazareth—because his project was soul-sized, and so it awakened the soul, which in turned roused Herod. "Fear not," as in, "Bring consciousness to your fears. Set them in the context of this sacred vocation: to identify with your bigger, Christ-loving, Spirit-called, all-consuming passion for the Holy."

This Christmas story is an invitation to trust the wisdom and guidance of your inner Magi. They will lead you to the stable. The final detail of the story is that after the Magi visit the Christ child, "they left for their own country by another road." That "other road" is a pretty good definition of what it means to be church.

Losing the Veil

Exodus 34:29-35, 2 Corinthians 3:12-4:2, Luke 9:28-36

These Scripture readings deal, in one way or another, with the "problem" of radiance. By radiance, I mean simply the presence or light of God that shines out of all creation, including you and me. It's not really a problem for us when we see it in creation—the flash of a red-winged blackbird's wing against the blue sky, the morning sun on the snow-laden mountains across the Burrard Inlet, dusk's light revealing the stunning beauty of a tree you've walked by a thousand times without noticing it. These we regard as simple, beautiful blessings of the Creator. "The world," wrote the poet Gerard Manley Hopkins, "is charged with the grandeur of God."[1]

The problem begins when that same radiance, the glory of God, shines out of human beings. We don't know what to make of it or do with it. Take the story from Exodus. Moses goes up a mountain to commune with the Holy One and returns with a beaming countenance, which you'd think would be an unambiguously good thing. But see what happens? Moses talks with the people, so they see the radiance. But then, before it wears off, Moses covers his face with a veil and then goes back up the mountain to get recharged. What's going on?

What's at stake in this passage is Moses's authority as a leader. His radiance is what convinces the people that he really is God's

---

[1] Gerard Manley Hopkins, "God's Grandeur," *God's Grandeur and Other Poems* (Toronto: General Publishing Company, Ltd., 1995), 15.

representative and is fit to lead them. But Moses knows that this is a finicky lot. They've already come close to offing him because things didn't go quite according to their plans. Moses is keenly aware that his authority as a leader, and perhaps his very life, depends upon his personal wattage. So before the shining wears off, he puts a veil over his face. Notice that radiance is believed to be located exclusively here in a chosen individual. He's got the glory and so he's got the responsibility. And the people like it that way.[2]

Something about this passage from Exodus resonated with the early Christian community, because both Paul and then the gospel writers do theological riffs on the story. In the gospel story, known as the transfiguration (Luke 9:28–36), Jesus takes three disciples up the mountain and has a chat with two Jewish prophets, Moses and Elijah. Jesus's radiance, apparently, is overwhelming. Then, when Moses and Elijah disappear, Peter suggests building three booths, one for each of the prophets. But the writer of the story says that Peter didn't know what he was saying, that his mistake was putting Jesus on par with the other two prophets. Peter should have noticed, according to the gospel tradition, that Jesus's radiance was brighter and more enduring.

Here again, like in the story of Moses going up the mountain, the writer of the gospel suggests that the light of the transfiguration belongs to Jesus alone. The disciples should be listening to *him*, and not the other two. Once more, radiance is located exclusively in the leader—Jesus of Nazareth. It's like there's not enough radiance to go around.

But Paul gets it. He takes the same passage from Exodus and comes to a radically different conclusion—namely, "All of us, with unveiled faces, seeing the glory of the Lord as though reflected in a mirror, are being transformed into the same image from one degree of glory to another; for this comes from the Lord, the Spirit" (2 Corinthians 3:18).

"All of us." There's the key. Holy radiance doesn't just shine out

---

[2] This is my interpretation of Paul at 2 Corinthians 3:12–13: "Since, then, we have such a hope, we act with great boldness, not like Moses, who put a veil over his face to keep the people of Israel from gazing at the end of the glory."

of special individuals, chosen by God. God doesn't work that way. We're all chosen, all full of glory, all in the process of being transformed "from one degree of glory to another." So let's toss the veils. "Let it shine, let it shine, let it shine," as the children's song goes. This journey through time is about being transformed by the same image that shone from Christ, from one degree of glory to another. We're meant to evolve in our capacity for radiance—that's the spiritual path. As if reading our minds and hearing our protests, Paul assures us that this radiance comes from Spirit (3:18). In other words, it's not about our little selves, so get over it.

This is the little secret that we keep even from ourselves: we like the arrangement by which only certain others are specially called. It lets us off the hook. We'll let *them* shine. Some congregations make a habit of this. If they perceive that the minister's light is not shining quite brightly enough, so much for their leader. We like the light being located in someone else. When it stops shining, we have a scapegoat. Before we get all worked up over whether Canadian Muslim women should wear a veil or not, let's first ask if we ourselves wear the veil that keeps our radiance from shining out. It's a lot easier to hide behind the veil and call it humility than to tear it off and let the Mind and Heart of the Christ shine through us.

I've had a taste of what it's like to go from one degree of glory to another. It's terrifying, because the more light that comes through, the more exposed you feel—there's no hiding. I'm currently in a phase of my life when Spirit seems to be calling me to light it up, to go public, write books, lead public talks and workshops, and speak out about an evolutionary Christian faith—not from the safety of my own sanctuary, not preaching to the choir, but out in public, where they eat Christians alive! Okay, I'm exaggerating a bit. At least, I hope I'm exaggerating. God is calling me to let my light shine, but here's the thing: if it were all about the little me, I'd be sunk. But it's not my light, not my little personal self. It's the light of Christ consciousness, or the light of Spirit—Paul says that they are the same thing (3:18).

This is where our little self gets tripped up. We've been told that it's Christian to be modest and humble. We've learned to associate humility with low wattage. But if it's really not about us—if we really get that it's about Spirit shining through the person that we call me—then humility means getting out of the way of the radiant Spirit. Who are we *not* to let the light shine? And that's frightening. And the reason it's frightening is that when my little self tries to convince me that it *is* about me, then I start thinking things like, "I'm not smart enough. I'll blow it. I'll be criticized." You know the voice. And then the still, small voice of Christ whispers, "Get over yourself. Let it flow. Get out of the way."

That's why I go with Paul's take on the matter. Each of us is a centre of divine radiance. We are called to go from one degree of glory to another—Spirit's glory, Christ's radiance. Jesus invites all of us up the mountain, not to build booths or any other monument to him or anybody else. He takes us up there so that we can get a glimpse of the glory that shines out from all of us. The same light that shines in Christ shines still today through willing souls.

An Evolutionary Take on Sin

Romans 6:12–16

Within days of the Vancouver riot that followed game seven of the NHL final series in 2011, just about everybody had weighed in on it. The causes given ranged from the mundane—this is just what twenty-something-year-old men do when they get a chance—to in-depth sociological analyses of mob behaviour. But nobody talked about it being the result of "sin." If Paul were around, he might have used the riot as a prime example of sin exercising "dominion in [our] mortal bodies, to make [us] obey [sin's] passions" (Romans 6:12). In the modern era, the only institution that even uses the word *sin* to account for bad behaviour is the church. I wonder if the word has outlived its usefulness.

For Paul, sin was a mysterious external force. Sin was imagined to be an entity that enjoyed agency. It made him do stuff he didn't want to do. The good that Paul wants to do, he doesn't do, and the evil that he wants to refrain from doing is the very thing he does (Romans 7:19). He was a man undone by the power of sin working through his bodily passions. Sin exercises dominion (6:12); it causes spiritual death (6:13); sin is a master whom we serve (6:16). For Paul, there was a spiritual war going on between the power of sin to enslave us, and the power of God to liberate us for eternal life.

When I became a Christian, the first step was to admit that I was a sinner. I was told to memorize this verse of Scripture: "all have sinned and fall short of the glory of God" (Romans 3:23). I had to generate a list of all the bad things I had ever done, in order to prove the point. The worst sin I could come up with was that I stole some cutlery from the restaurant where I was waiting on tables. Once that was established (that I was, by nature, sinful), then the need for Jesus was clear. He died to take my sin away. If I believed that, I was saved for eternal life. If you didn't admit that you were a sinner, there was no real need for Jesus. There was a lot riding on getting me to believe that I was irredeemably fallen.

One of Christ's primary roles, in Paul's theology, is to set us free from sin. Before Christ, all that Paul had to keep him from succumbing to this mysterious force was the Law. There were rules of behaviour, rules about what to eat, rules about when and how to pray, rules about whom to spent time with, rules about what women could wear, rules about how to treat animals and how to treat each other, and rules about religious rituals and sacrifices. And, of course, where there are rules, there are also consequences. Strict adherence to these rules and the consequences for breaking them were what distinguished the Jewish people from the rest of society. Indeed, Jews were known for being highly ethical people.

But for Paul, these rules weren't enough. He was a Pharisee, an orthodox Jew, who strictly followed the Law. All that the Laws accomplished in the end was convicting him of the power of sin, because on the inside, the impulses and the instincts—which caused his body to be one of the "instruments of wickedness"—didn't go away. They just went underground, and they came back to torment him.

A person named Dayna who responded to a blog post I wrote on sin once heard a professor say that sin was like Johnsongrass (in Vancouver the analogy might be goutweed): you dig it out by the root and think you have it all, but the next spring it will grow back, no matter what you do.

And it needs to be said that those early converts to Christianity never seemed to be absolutely liberated from this mysterious force.

The roots were so deep that it kept coming back. Paul's letter to the Romans in Romans 6:12–16 is a warning about sin. Since he was warning about the power of sin, it was obviously because some in the community were continuing to behave as though they were slaves to sin and not to righteousness. It seems that neither the Law nor life in Christ was able to root out this powerful force.

Whatever we call it, the behaviours associated with sin are still with us today. Politicians and powerful men—like former International Monetary Fund chief Dominique Strauss-Kahn and former U.S. congressman Anthony Weiner—are just recent examples of powerful men risking or ruining their careers for sex. Elite athletes, like Tiger Woods and Kobe Bryant, succumb to temptation. Dictators continue to slaughter their own people for the sake of power. We are wreaking havoc on our ecological systems. We succumb to every imaginable form of addiction. Priests sexually act out with children. We seem to be slaves to sin. You can understand why Paul imagined sin to be an external power with agency—as though it had an agenda to keep us enslaved.

Clearly, being Christian is not the magic bullet for eliminating sin. Has anything changed in two thousand years? Or are we forever destined to engage in behaviour that keeps us doing really unintelligent and destructive things?

Some things have changed. Paul had no way of knowing, for example, that we are evolutionary creatures. He had to piece together his theology and worldview in a prescientific era. But ever since Darwin's discovery of natural selection, we've known that we are connected to every creature that ever preceded us. The bugs and the birds, the reptiles and the mammals are all carried inside of us all of the time. We inherited our physical shape, our physiology, and our instincts. We may be distinct from our animal kin, but we are not separate from them. The reptile's fundamental concerns are with sex, survival, and security. Our mammalian ancestors incorporated these impulses and instincts, and added to them the instinct to belong and to acquire status. Our early human ancestors gave us the instinct to interpret reality, to form patterns of meanings, and to connect the past with the present and the future. These instincts and impulses are mediated through three distinct, but connected, brains that are stacked on top of each other inside our craniums.

Most of the behaviour that the Bible calls sinful originates from these primitive urges that are associated with our brains, which then trigger the release of hormones. This is why a man with high testosterone sees a beautiful woman and is positive that she should be carrying his baby. We also know that increased testosterone in the male is associated with higher status. Elite athletes, CEOs, presidents, and clergy are the first to get into trouble. A recent promotion at work will fire off a release of testosterone, making us vulnerable to sexual acting out. Or, if somebody does something that we perceive to be a threat, our *amygdala*—a gland associated with the fight-or-flight response—will release hormones. Whomever we perceive to be a threat, including our loved ones, will immediately appear to us as the enemy. This is what Michael Dowd calls our "Lizard Legacy."[1] If I perceive my wife to be a threat, my neocortex will actually help me rationalize turning her into an enemy. I'll come up with all kinds of arguments that justify my perception that she is out to get me.

Paul knew none of this. What Paul imagined to be a war between his "members" was actually going on between his ears. His lower nature (or let's call it his earlier nature) hijacked his spiritual commitments to living a morally good life. Without the benefit of science, Paul had no way to integrate or take ownership of these forces. He projected them outward. He felt as though he were being attacked. Today we know that sin is an inside job.

This scientific knowledge of the evolutionary nature of human be-

---

[1] Michael Dowd, *Thank God for Evolution: How the Marriage of Science and Religion Will Transform Your Life and Our World* (Toronto: Penguin Group, 2007).

ings radically alters our strategy for dealing with sin. We're not going to try to expunge it from our system—an impossible task because it's simply a part of us that's not going anywhere. We could meditate for thirty years, and when we came out of the meditation, these earlier instincts would still get triggered. And if we think we are above such impulses, they will rise up and bite us in the butt. Beware of gurus and dewy-eyed spiritual masters who believe that they have exorcised their inner crocodile. That is, itself, a "croc"! They will end up exhibiting the need for status, assuming that all women exist for their sexual pleasure, and amassing enormous quantities of personal wealth to satiate their need for security. And they will call it abundance consciousness.

Stricter moral codes and believing in Jesus are not strategies for dealing with sin in the twenty-first century. Instead, we must learn how our brain works and bring conscious awareness to our behaviour. Our brains, hormones, and biochemistry are gifts of our evolutionary kin. *They are not the enemy. But neither are they meant to be the master.*

In his book *Thank God for Evolution*, Michael Dowd uses the example of the elephant and its rider. The elephant represents our instincts. The rider represents our rational mind, which we think is in control. But if the elephant decides to veer off the path we've set, we'll soon find out that we're not in absolute control. As we know, one of the functions of the neocortex is to interpret reality to justify our belief that we are in control of the elephant. Psychoanalysts call this thinking rationalization. And we now know that our capacity for self-deceit has evolutionary advantages. It helped us to survive. The trick, it seems, is learning to be in a conscious relationship with the elephant, and giving the elephant enough of what it needs and wants so that it doesn't become our pilot.

Paul was right about this much: either we'll be slaves to our instincts, or we will learn to manage them and take responsibility for our lives. Despite scientific knowledge, most of the human race is held hostage by our instincts for security, status, and sex. To break free, the first step is to develop a witnessing relationship to them—not to get rid of them, that is, just to learn to notice them without identifying with them. We need to learn that we have these instincts, but that they don't have us. We also know that our prefrontal lobes are associated with the capacity to do the harder thing and make the difficult choice. We are not at the mercy of our earlier instincts.

Paul, the mystic, exhorted the early church to "Let the same mind be in [us] that was in Christ Jesus" (Philippians 2:5). This mind is a higher mind, which helps us know that we are one with All That Is, including Spirit. This higher mind is also correlated with our prefrontal lobes and the right hemisphere of our bilateral brain. This oneness (or unitive consciousness) keeps us aware that a whole universe exists within us. Our role is to take responsibility for how we show up. This higher mind—Christ consciousness—grasps that we are proof of the universe evolving, and that our prime directive is not to follow the dictates of the ancient past, but to harness the energy of these instincts so that they might serve a new future, which Jesus called the Kin(g)dom or Realm of God.

We're not sinners. We're evolutionary creatures who are learning to be grateful for our earliest instincts, and to integrate them into a more evolved expression of what it means to be fully human.

Assisted Migration

Luke 4:16-30

This passage from Luke's gospel represents Jesus's mission statement. It's Jesus's turn to be the lay reader at the worship service. The text for the morning is from the prophet Isaiah. Jesus stands before his friends and family and the good people of his local village, and delivers the reading. You can imagine his parents being proud of the way he read. There is general agreement that he reads with understanding. A few even think that someday he might make a good local rabbi.

But nobody is prepared for what comes next. It isn't a long and eloquent sermon. It is a *one-liner* that ultimately leads to consternation in the congregation. Jesus finishes the reading, rolls up the scroll, and gives it back to the attendant. Then he sits down. (Are you picking up the drama here?) All the eyes of the synagogue are on him. Then he delivers the shortest sermon on record: "Today, this Scripture has been fulfilled in your hearing" (Luke 4:21).

Because I'm not nearly the preacher that Jesus was, my sermons take a little longer to flesh out!

The backstory to this event is that Jesus had just come back from forty days in the wilderness, where he fought twelve rounds with his inner demons. He was sorting out the voice of Spirit from the voices in his head that came from his little self. Was he in this for the power, fame, and money? Or was his life about something else? After forty days and forty nights of discernment, Jesus's little self had given way to a much-expanded Self. He had discovered and consented to his deep purpose.

So by the time he stands up to deliver Isaiah's words, "The Spirit of the Lord is upon me," the Spirit of the Lord actually *was* upon him. The reason people were so moved by the reading is that the familiar words carried Spirit's power.

Effectively, Jesus was announcing that he was the living embodiment of Isaiah's vision. He was so identified with his higher spiritual calling that when people heard him read the words, they knew that Jesus was saying: "This is happening through me. I've been anointed to bring good news to the poor, to proclaim release to the captives and the recovery of sight to the blind, and to let the oppressed go free."

I'm less interested in what Jesus's calling was than I am in his willingness to own it so deeply that everybody who heard him read those words knew that he was stepping up and saying: "This is what my life is for."

We hear this story and think that Jesus must have been a pretty amazing guy—so much conviction, such an exceptional human being. In fact, he's so amazing that we should worship Jesus or, if we're more progressive, at least admire his leadership capacity. He's so exceptional that we should put him on a pedestal—way up there beyond the rest of us.

But wait just a minute, isn't that the life that the devil offered him out in the desert? Isn't that what Jesus rejected?

Although Jesus rejected that offer, Christian churches all across the world do it anyway. Is that what Jesus would have wanted? Does putting Jesus up on a pedestal let us off the hook? If Jesus were alive today, wouldn't he tell us to do our own time in the wilderness until we emerge with a clear sense of our larger identity and calling? He might encourage us to complete that sentence from Isaiah for ourselves: "The Spirit of the Lord is upon me, because he has anointed me to. . ." It's the Christian vocation to complete the sentence. I suspect that Jesus would trade all the veneration he's received throughout the ages to know that we who read this story go beyond admiration and reverence, and actually answer that question for ourselves.

Julia Butterfly Hill spent 738 consecutive days and nights living in an old-growth redwood tree to prevent it from being cut down by the Pacific Lumber Company. How do you spend two years living in a tree and *never* come down? Well, using Isaiah's language, "The Spirit of the Lord" was upon her. Julia might rather say, "The Spirit of the redwood forest" was upon her. The language is not nearly as important as finding what will elevate you beyond the mere impulse to survive.

There is something undignified about human beings in the twenty-first century, especially in the affluent nations of the world, how we are still organizing our lives around survival—still living as though we'll never have enough, still living to fulfil our personal pleasures, still defending ourselves against every other person as though they represent a threat to our survival, still thinking that money is the key to the meaning of life. Jesus went to the desert without any food, and realized he could trust the universe to provide; he went without any money, and realized that there is a distinction between money and true wealth; he went without any fame or social status, and realized that his soul had lost interest in that game. He found his tree.

I'm not saying that we all have to do something as dramatic as live in a redwood tree or get ourselves crucified for a cause. Identifying the deep purposes of your life is a lifelong project, and it evolves over time. I go back over my life and identify, decade by decade, what I thought my life was for. It has evolved. At one time, my deep purpose was to be the best athlete that I could be at whatever sport I was playing. Then it was to find the meaning of life. This evolved into helping others discover their meaning in life (and during this period, I grew a beard, trying to look like Jesus!). Then my tree became integrating Christianity with the great evolving story of the universe. Now my purpose is to help reinvent Christianity by bringing an evolutionary paradigm to bear on the Christian tradition. None of these declarations of my tree were lost with the emergence of the next; rather, each formed the foundation for the next iteration.

And in each case, it was less a matter of sitting down and asking myself, "Okay, what will the Spirit of God be upon me to do in this decade?"; it was more about following my deep allurements and discovering what my life was for in each moment.

A central feature of the spiritual life is this wrestling to discover and declare, as best we can at any given moment in time, the purpose of our lives.

There truly isn't a one-size-fits-all answer to the question of life's purpose. For some, the Spirit is upon them to be the most loving parents or partners they can be. Other people might feel called to be the most creative entrepreneurs they can imagine—and to use their wealth to change the world in some way. One way to discover your purpose for yourself is to take an honest look at your life as it exists right now and ask yourself where your fire is. What makes your heart burn with passion? Then find a way to do it with all your heart and soul and mind. And don't judge it—as though your passion doesn't measure up to a good-enough passion. Just live it.

The other day, I had a cup of tea with a friend and he managed to keep from yawning while I complained about how busy I was. The next day, he sent me a one-line email: "Know your business." It was an invitation to reorient myself around my deep calling. I suspect that if we're always complaining of being too busy, it's because we're distracted by stuff that isn't any of our business.

Connie Barlow, an evolutionary biologist and journalist, is involved in a grassroots movement of lay horticulturalists. They look for species of trees and other plants that are at risk in their native bioregion because of climate change, and then they transplant them to different regions that are more supportive of their growth. This is something that happens naturally in evolution, but it takes vast periods of time.

With humans acting on their behalf, it can be done in weeks. They call it assisted migration.

That's a perfect description of the task of my community that teaches and practises evolutionary Christian spirituality. That's our tree—assisted migration. We assist the migrations of souls who aren't thriving. The bioregion of modern culture is ill suited to thriving, growing souls because it tries to convince us that we're nothing but a collection of consumers. We transport the at-risk souls to another kind of soil, another spiritual bioregion, that is more conducive to the evolution of the big Self. We assist their migration to more all-encompassing regions of consciousness so that they can see the true significance and purpose of their life.

The Spirit of the Lord is upon us to assist the migration of willing souls into landscapes and regions of the Spirit, so that they can discover the divine within them and make a difference in the world out of that deep identity. Who wouldn't want to be part of that project?

Easter: Idle Tale or Love's Testament?

Luke 24:1-12

We'll never know whether or not Jesus physically rose from the dead. If there were a video camera inside the tomb, would its recording have shown a man getting up and removing his grave clothes, or perhaps some kind of spiritual, etheric body rising up like a mist and exiting the tomb? We have no way of knowing. All we have are the reports of the gospel writers who wrote their stories decades after Jesus was crucified. All we have are stories.

Stories, for example, of women reporting that Jesus's body was missing and then strangers reminding them that Jesus had said that rising from the grave on the third day was part of the deal. According to the writer of Luke's gospel, at first the disciples thought it was "an idle tale." What were they supposed to believe? Their own eyes had witnessed Jesus's brutal execution. But maybe they believed this story of Love triumphing over violence and death itself. Much depends on the stories we believe, consciously or unconsciously. In fact, what we call reality appears to us within the context of the stories we hold to be true.

The most important stories are the ones we may not even be aware of. These are the Big Stories or what some people call cultural worldviews. We inherit these Big Stories without knowing it. They subliminally tell us what to believe and value, the nature of God, and the purpose of life. They act like glasses, focusing our attention and determining what we see.

When the women returned from the tomb on that first Easter with a great story to tell about the tomb being empty and angels telling them that Jesus had risen, what kinds of glasses were the disciples wearing to help them make sense of this story? One of the Big Stories that has determined what men are able to see is the story of patriarchy. This is a story that has unconsciously shaped our take on reality throughout most of history and still is assumed by the majority of the world's population. In the first century, women were not reliable witnesses in a court of law. These male disciples were not predisposed to take a woman's word for it—about this or anything else important.

Another Big Story that had the disciples confused was their story of God. On the one hand, their faith told them that God was all-powerful and in charge of history. On the other hand, they had just witnessed their spiritual leader's crucifixion, at the hands of Caesar. So, who was in charge of history, God or Caesar? They were experiencing a clash of narratives. Imagine having witnessed a crucifixion and then hearing a few days later that the guy who was crucified is alive. It's bound to be a little confusing. It must have been an idle tale. Caesar just finished crushing God.

This story that the women brought to them was hard to believe—a story implying that Love is stronger than violence, that life is the context for death, and that the kind of humanity that Jesus represented could not be snuffed out by the kind of human being that had executed him. That's the Easter story in a nutshell, and now I'm asking you which story you're going to believe: the story of death or the story of life; the story of God affirming human dignity or God abandoning us to the worst in us. Christ is risen: Idle tale or Love's testament?

Here's another seemingly unbelievable story, this one from *The Empathic Civilization* by Jeremy Rifkin, a popular social thinker. The setting is World War I, the bloodiest war in the history of humanity. This story is said to have happened on December 24, 1914. The Germans and the Allied soldiers were in their respective trenches, in some place no more than twenty-five yards away from each other. They were wet and cold. Dead bodies were scattered among the living. Rats and vermin skittered about their feet.

As dusk fell, the German soldiers lit candles and set them upon small Christmas trees that had been sent to offer comfort to the men. Some began to sing Christmas carols—first "Silent Night" and then others. The Allied forces applauded at the end of each carol. Then the English soldiers started in with their favourite hymns and received robust applause from the Germans. A few men from the English side went up over the trenches into no man's land. More followed. Soon thousands of English and Germans met on middle ground. They shook hands, hugged, and exchanged cigarettes. Soccer games sprung up. This went on until dawn. Some reports say that as many as 100,000 enemies met in no man's land that night, and became friends—men, who hours before had been trying to kill each other, joined in celebration of the Christmas story about the birth of Love.[1]

Idle tale? More than 8.5 million soldiers perished in this war, and yet for one evening, these mortal enemies put down their weapons and allowed their common humanity to win out. To me, this story is every bit as miraculous as the Easter story.

Many people have come to the conclusion that the only non-idle tale is the story of humanity's depravity. These people are ardent believers in Good Friday. If you want a true portrait of the human being, they tell us, look at what the Romans did to Jesus; humanity is, by nature, violent, self-centred, and greedy. What happened on Christmas Eve of 1914, they assure us, was an aberration. The next day, the generals of both sides got wind of what had happened, and they moved quickly to end the freakish show of humanity. The killing resumed. That's the true story of humanity that they ask us to believe.

---

[1] Jeremy Rifkin, *The Empathetic Civilization: The Race to Global Consciousness in a World in Crisis* (New York: Penguin Group, Inc., 2009), 5–6.

Christians have been telling themselves that story for centuries—it's the story of original sin. We are fallen creatures, and only a supernatural act of God can save us. We are bad, and God alone is good. Good Friday should surprise nobody, according to this tale. It's this Easter story that is an idle tale—a product of wishful, romantic thinking.

As Rifkin points out in his book, "At the cusp of the modern era, the British philosopher Thomas Hobbes quipped that 'the life of man [is] solitary, poor, nasty, brutish, and short.'"[2] John Locke, an English philosopher, was convinced that humans were acquisitive by nature. We grasp hold of anything and anybody that we can, and mould the other to meet our selfish needs. And we need to maximize this impulse, conquering nature and turning its wasteland into something more productive.

Adam Smith, the father of modern capitalism, believed that the economic system was fuelled by little more than self-interest. His philosophy was more nuanced (and moral) than what it spawned in the form of neoliberal economic philosophy, but it was based in the same fundamental belief in our selfish instincts. Modern-day atheists use Darwin's theory of evolution to reinforce this idea of a purposeless existence, since our survival is a result of thoughtless manipulation of genetic material. The father of psychology, Sigmund Freud, carried on this line of thought, concluding that the human being is a pleasure-seeking organism, struggling to control our base instincts.

A big cultural story about the nature of human beings gets frozen at the Good Friday execution of Jesus. Our media reinforce this story. The newsworthy is whatever is violent, tragic, and brutal. This is the story that we have come to believe. When an Easter story is introduced into this narrative, we, like those first disciples, have an impulse to call it an idle tale.

Although we keep telling ourselves about our own depravity, an emerging science of empathy is showing that human beings are ac-

---

[2] Ibid., 7.

tually empathic by nature. Dr. Barbara King, chancellor professor of anthropology at the College of William and Mary, studies apes and monkeys in the wild and in captivity. She is convinced that the religious instinct has its evolutionary origins in the impulse to belong. To feel as though we belong, we need an Other, a Thou, to love us into being, to show us that we have a place in the universe. Many observers of apes and gorillas see only the alpha behaviour of males, and the aggressive instinct. That is certainly present in these animals. But what King also sees from these beautiful creatures are elaborate nurturing rituals. The need to belong, through rituals of love, is built into the fabric of our evolutionary being.[3]

This need is deeper than any other instinct, including survival. For example, in an experiment performed at the University of Wisconsin in 1958, Harry Harlow and his team of researchers deprived infant monkeys of their mothers. They set up two artificial surrogate mothers. One of them was simply chicken wire wrapped around a frame, with a nipple that dispensed milk. The other surrogate was wrapped with soft cloth and warmed by radiant heat. The infants chose the softer, warmer "mother" 100% of the time. But the researchers took it one step further. They set it up so that only the surrogate mother made of cold chicken wire dispensed milk. They were shocked to discover that the infant monkeys chose the soft, warm surrogate that gave them no milk over the cold chicken-wire surrogate that dispensed milk. They persisted in this choice to the point of death.[4]

Life, it seems, is not primarily about survival. It's about feeling a sense of belonging. In the human realm, this need to belong evolves. It begins first with the mother, then with the nuclear family, then with peers, then with one's nation and ethnic group, then with all of humanity, and finally with the entire cosmos. In the religious or spiritu-

---

[3] Barbara J. King, *Evolving God: A Provocative View on the Origins of Religion* (New York: Doubleday, 2007), 1–9.

[4] Rifkin, *Empathic Civilization*, 18–19.

ally inclined, there is an intuition that the entire universe is unfolding within the heart of God. God, then, is the intuition of the Beloved Other—the one who holds us, nurtures us, and nourishes us into being. The essence of the spiritual life is the realization and cultivation of this deep intuition that we belong—to each other, to the planet, to the universe, and to God, who holds it all, and hold us all, to Her breast.

It just may turn out that the idle tale is the story of Good Friday told as though it's the complete story, without the last chapter of Easter. Jeremy Rifkin suggests that the reason that crucifixion, tragedy, and violence stand out is that they are deviations from the norm. The media counts on tales of woe to catch our attention. And the very reason they catch our attention is that most of us, most of the time, are not sitting around plotting to murder our neighbours, let alone execute them. Most of us, most of the time, are relating to others, trying to be kind, looking for ways to socialize and connect, empathizing with the plight of others when they're going through tough times. We're connecting because we want to belong, and that's mostly what human beings do. And now, it has dawned on scientists that we should study feelings like belonging, empathy, connectedness, and love, because these feelings might be primary characteristics of what it means to be human.

It turns out that those soldiers on Christmas Eve of 1914, were doing what has come naturally to human beings for 200,000 years and, even before Homo sapiens sapiens emerged, what was natural for apes to do for millions of years. We had to be socialized to hate each other.

The Easter story of Jesus being raised from the dead is the story that is the larger context for Good Friday. Bad things happen, yes. Tragedy and suffering and violence are part of the story of what it means to be human. The history of violence could be told as the history of men who have cut themselves off emotionally from cultures of belonging.

But we reach out for love, and we offer love, because, as the author of the first letter of John puts it, God "first loved us" (1 John 4:19). God loves the whole cosmos into being. Since we're made in

God's image, we love, we find ways to belong, and we work to enlarge the circle of belonging on the planet Earth. It's taken the evolutionary process to awaken to this fundamental characteristic of the universe, but now scientists are discovering that we're hard-wired for love. We all know that life means nothing without love, and the reason so many, for so many years, have been attracted to Jesus is that he was the heart of God in human form.

So the real story is that we're evolving in and toward the heart of God. To say that Jesus rose from the grave is to tell the Big Story that you can't kill Love. You can't kill Love because you can't kill God. God just is. Crucify God, and God will rise up. Put human beings across from each other in trenches and order them to kill each other, but on Christmas Eve, love will rise up. The direction of the evolutionary process is always toward widening circles of love and belonging. This is where Love is going, and nothing can stop it. Love's resurrection is just part of the deal.

And here's the thing: if you feel full of despair and disappointment, if you are convinced that your life is at a dead end and that circumstances have rolled a stone across the tomb of your life, if you feel like you're finished with love, Love is not finished with you. You might feel like you don't belong, but don't believe that story. You belong. You belong to God. Give love half a chance, and Love will reach into the darkness of your soul and raise you from the grave. This comes with a money-back guarantee. Because this is just what Love does. Because you are born from the heart of God, into the heart of God, and you are evolving into the heart of God. All you have to do is open to reality, and Love will raise you up.

They crucified Love. Yes. We are still crucifying Love today. Who can deny it? But you can't kill Love. It rises up and sends *us* out to be the resurrected heart of God for the world. This is no idle tale. Christ is risen. Hallelujah!

Power Plays

1 Kings 21:1-21, Luke 7:36-8:3

When we look at the evolutionary development of the universe, it is undeniable that human beings have become what cosmological physicist Dr. Brian Swimme calls a "macrophase" power of the planet.[1] We are not merely one power among others. We have become the species upon whom the future of the planet depends.

The universe has arrived at a species that literally embodies a sacred power—the power to influence the entire planetary system with how we exercise our power or how we refuse to exercise our power. This is a relatively recent development—perhaps in the last three hundred years, but more significantly in the last few decades. By the timetable of the cosmic clock, this magnification of power in a single species happened only a second ago. The most essential thing that we can do for our future is to become conscious of how we use our power and assume radical responsibility for this gift. We can no longer afford to pretend that we are not responsible for the quality of life on our planet. Life literally hangs in the balance—the life of our soul and the life of our planet.

Let's look at different forms of power through the lens of each of the characters in the biblical readings: King Ahab; Queen Jezebel; Naboth, the farmer; Elijah, the prophet; Mary, the prostitute; and Jesus, the anointed one.

---

[1] Brian Swimme, *The Hidden Heart of the Cosmos: Humanity and the New Story* (New York: Orbis Books, 1996).

Power of Passivity

In 1 King 21:1–21, King Ahab displays power as passivity. He appears to be powerless, and yet we see in him the disastrous consequences of the passive exercise of power. He wants Naboth's vineyard for his own vegetable garden, and when Naboth refuses, he goes home, pulls a blankie over his head, and sulks. He acts helpless in the face of rejection. He might have organized a team of his subjects to go out and knock on the doors of all the vineyard owners and offer them the same deal. He might have first accepted the conditions of his life—that his first try was a rejection—and then come up with ten alternative ways to solve his problem. How this guy got to be king is beyond me, but there he is.

We all have an inner Ahab. Self psychologist Robert Kegan calls the toddler's stage of development the "impulsive self;"[2] this is the royal self that assumes that the world exists to meet our needs, and when it doesn't, we collapse in a heap of helplessness. It's fine in a two-year-old but most distasteful in grown-ups. We collapse in ourselves, our creative agency completely shuts down, and we deem the world to be against us. The mantra of this exercise of power is: "What can you do?" (except sulk or throw a tantrum).

When this power is exercised in adults, we get other people to make decisions on our behalf, and, thereby, we are never required to take responsibility. Our passivity elicits rescuer behaviour in others who themselves need to justify their existence by being useful. This is convenient for the passive Ahab in us because when it doesn't go so well, we can blame them. It is a strategy in the service of avoiding responsibility for our life. It only appears like powerlessness. In truth, it is a passive exercise of power.

As humans spiritually evolve, we increase our capacity to assume radical responsibility for the conditions of our lives, individually and collectively. Passivity is the refusal of this evolutionary directive.

---

[2] Robert Kegan, *The Evolving Self: Problem and Process in Human Development* (Cambridge: Harvard University Press, 1982), 133.

Power as Domination

I recently skimmed through one of those name-your-baby books and didn't find one reference to Jezebel. Queen Jezebel suffers from the polar opposite of her cowardly husband. She knows what to do with her power—use it to take exactly what she wants from this world, and do so without guilt or shame. She takes her place in a long line of women who compensate for weak men.

She arranges for the murder of Naboth in order to seize his land so that it can become a royal vegetable garden for her husband. In the emergence of historical worldviews and the self, this act is an example of the part of us that distinguishes itself through domination. It's the bully self or the bully race—the warrior who takes exactly what she, or more typically he, wants.

We have been turning indigenous lands into vegetable gardens for thousands of years—the practice still continues. Replace vegetable gardens with exports like sugar, coffee plantations, gold and diamonds mines. We want your productive land that feeds you so that we can use it to export crops and get rich. We want to take the legacy of a 13.7-billion-year-old planet and possess and exploit what never belonged to us in the first place. We take exactly what we want and do so shamelessly. The death and violence that is spreading like oil in the Gulf of Mexico is an expression of Jezebel energy. We'll take exactly what we want, any way we can get it, and hang the potential consequences.

This Jezebel energy is within us in our relationships as well. Whenever we don't see and validate our loved ones as distinct from us, with their own unique needs and wants, we are metaphorically planting our vegetable garden in the ancestral soil of their dignity. The ones we say we love can be little more than fulfillers of our deficiency needs. We *take* from them rather than consciously negotiating what we want from a place of vulnerability, which would mean that we would need to *receive* their gifts with gratitude—not unconsciously expropriate them.

Like Ahab, we need Jezebel to do our dirty work. The European colonizers gave me the land that my home now sits on. It once belonged to the Burrard Nation—but thanks to those conquerors, I can sleep pretty well at night, knowing that I didn't *personally* take the land. We need BP to be the scapegoat in the 2010 oil spill into the Gulf of Mexico. *We* didn't drill the oil without a backup plan. They did it. We just use the oil. We can picket BP gas stations, but picketing is a convenient distraction for the Ahab in us while we continue to fill up our tanks and gorge on fossil fuels. I wonder what would happen if we took responsibility for our own Jezebel. Make no mistake, the Jezebels of the world need to be called to account—including BP, along with the insanity of the oil and gas industry. But let's be honest and realize that we're wedded to Jezebel.

Power as Integrity

Naboth represents power as integrity. Naboth knows where he's rooted. He has a deep attachment to his ancestral land. His soul knows every inch of soil, and every rock and vine. He *is* his land. The king approaches him with an offer. How do you say no to a king? How do you say no to a generous offer? He must have known when the king approached him that he wasn't just dealing with Ahab. He is saying no to the ruthless Jezebel as well, and that is a different kettle of fish.

What is it within you that is not up for sale? What is your non-negotiable? What are you so deeply rooted in that it is inconceivable that you would sell out for any amount of money? We are inundated from all sides with promises of a quick fortune, with the lure of luxury and the latest doodads—from cars to kitchen counters. Everything, we're led to believe, has its price. Or does it? Does our soul have a price?

I like to think that this is what church is about. It's meant to be a feast for the soul, to help us remember the sacred ground in which we're rooted. It's meant to remind us, as much as anything else, what we must say no to if we want to live in integrity. To know this is to possess a very rare and precious power. Naboth is our inner hero, willing to border and protect and salute the ancestral inheritance that is our soul.

Power to Speak Our Truth

Prophets emerged from within the Jewish tradition to monitor and challenge the presumption of absolute power within the monarchy. Kings needed to be reminded that God was in charge, not kings. Elijah speaks the truth to Ahab. Notice that Elijah doesn't go to Jezebel. He sees through Ahab's feigned helplessness and holds him accountable before God and before the people.

Recently, there have been some humorous critiques of the postmodernist, relativist tendency to end every statement with an interrogative inflection. This would be like Elijah going to Ahab and declaring: "Uh, dude, I think you did a bad thing?" Nobody will make a declarative statement for fear of offending somebody. We seem unwilling to speak our truth? Elijah doesn't suffer from this affliction as God's prophet. "Where dogs licked up the blood of Naboth, dogs will also lick up your blood" (1 Kings 21:19). That's pretty clear.

It's not that Elijah is unafraid. Shortly after confronting Ahab, he flees from Jezabel to the hills. He's scared to death. He speaks his truth in spite of his fear of Jezebel's power. By the way, this praise of Elijah isn't licence to dump our every judgment upon the world. But there are times to say it straight and clear. It's a lost art.

Power as Love

Let's shift to the story from Luke's gospel. The unnamed woman in the story exercises another kind of power. The inference is that she is a prostitute and is, therefore, unclean. She should not be out in public because, by the standards of the purity laws, her impurity is contagious. Those whom she touches are rendered likewise impure. But she displays the kind of contagion that Jesus is willing to catch. She exhibits the power of devotional love. Jesus draws the attention of the religious types, who were condemning her, to what they are missing: "she has shown great love" (Luke 7:47). We become in life what we mostly deeply love.

She recognizes in Jesus the face of her saviour, the very face of God, who has the power to make her whole. She holds nothing back. She bathes Jesus's feet with her tears and dries them with her hair. She has found her divine beloved. Her devotion is a kind of anointing of Jesus as Messiah—the word means "the anointed one." She sees in him what the religious authorities cannot see, or refuse to see, or have no need of in their lives.

We are uncomfortable in the United Church with this kind of display of devotion for Jesus—dismissing it as Jesusolatry. We leave that kind of explicit love of Jesus to the evangelicals. But Jesus has always been for Christians the personal face of God, the Beloved Thou, through whom God's love is poured out upon us. This practice of adoration is a healthy check for our inner Jezebel—who aspires to be in absolute control. In devotion, our Jezebel ego is brought to her knees, before a power that is infinitely greater than she is.

The ego can do many things, but it cannot make us whole, because, by nature, it isolates; it cannot heal us, because, by nature, it pretends to be self-sufficient; it cannot lift us up to live a transcendent purpose, because, by definition, such a purpose transcends the little self. So the power of integrity is that it helps us to name what we need to say no to. Devotional love for Jesus, or the Buddha, or a saint who bears for us the face of God, can help us discover what our soul wants to say yes to—the promise of new life and a new start sustained by the unconditional love of the one we are offering our devotion to. To be unafraid to love without reserve brings us closer to God than anything else. It is a power that brings us back to reality.

Power as Forgiveness

The final character in the two stories is Jesus himself. He displays his power as forgiveness. I want to expand our understanding of forgiveness in such a way that it includes the traditional notion of forgiving sins but also goes beyond it. The religious authorities are offended that Jesus assumes he has the power to forgive. "Who is this who even forgives sins?" (7:49).

Forgiveness is the refusal to allow the past to absolutely shape the future. When we bind ourselves to our transgressor, it saps our creative energy. Self-forgiveness and forgiveness of others is a spiritual strategy for keeping us focused on the future that wants to emerge, rather than on the little self that wants us to stay on the wheel of fate. Jesus releases this woman so that she can be bigger than what her culture made of her and what she made of herself. He releases her from the bonds of low expectations. She is liberated to create.

There is a divine dimension within our anointed Self that has the power to release us from our attachment to the past and allow us to become the people God is calling us to be.

We possess much power: the power of passivity, the power to dominate, the power of integrity, the power to speak our truth, the power to love God with all of our heart and mind, and the creative power of forgiveness. To be a disciple of Christ is to take responsibility for each of these expressions of power in the service of the Kin(g)dom of God.

Why Forgive?

Matthew 18:21–25

When Jesus tells the disciples that they need to forgive not just seven times but seven times seventy, he is telling them that forgiveness needs to become a way of life—a spiritual habit. We tend to associate forgiveness with those times in our lives when somebody hurts us, or hurts others. We've all heard remarkable stories of forgiveness that make us wonder how human beings are capable of such grace. Sermons are peppered with these kinds of stories of forgiveness and, indeed, they are powerful. I want to include this important understanding of forgiveness but also expand it. I'll say more about this later, but let's begin with a basic question: Why forgive?

As I briefly touched on in "Power Plays," forgiveness is a spiritual strategy for keeping our creative energies flowing. The universe creates, and given that we are the universe, consciously evolving, any practice that aligns us with creative energy aligns us with Reality. Refusing to forgive binds our creativity to the past. It's held hostage. We allow the original wound and suffering to have dominion over our life in the present. We devote creative energy to strategies of revenge. We imagine that by holding on to the pain, by being angry, by not letting it go, we are somehow holding that person accountable. The rest of the world might forget, might move on, but how will the world know how much I've been hurt if I just release it? The person who wounded me has no right to get away with it. They will be held accountable by the judge and jury that my life has become. But in the process, our creativity is frozen. On the other hand, when we choose to forgive, we gain the same Heart and Mind that was in Jesus of Nazareth (Philippians 2:5)—one who changed history with this strategy of forgiveness.

Margaret Visser, author of *Beyond Fate*, believes that forgiveness is the greatest gift that Christianity has given to the world.[1] It allows us to transform fate—the re-enactment of past in perpetuity—into destiny. Fate is the acceptance that the future is determined in an absolute fashion by what has occurred in the past. If you hurt me or my family, my fate and the fate of my family is to return the hurt. Much of human civilization, including the history of tribes and nations, has been fatalistically determined by unwillingness to forgive. Destiny is the triumph of the future over the past by heroic acts of creativity—creativity that is set free by forgiveness.

Think about Jesus's last act on the cross. When Jesus forgives his executors, it releases his followers to determine their own destiny instead of being locked into strategies of revenge. If we want to talk about his death as redemptive, then let his death be an affirmation that he redeemed us from the power of fate. He wasn't taking away the sins of the world. Nobody can actually do that. He was enacting a strategy for dealing with trauma—forgiveness. He was walking his talk. He taught forgiveness before his execution, and it became the final conscious choice of his life. In truth, his death was less redemptive than it was the triumph of creativity, as forgiveness is in the service of creation. This is why Paul talks about "a new creation" in Christ (2 Corinthians 5:17). The new creation that flowed out from the cross was made possible by his final and ultimate act of releasing his followers from the dictates and sovereignty of fate.

With this in mind, I want to expand the definition and understanding of forgiveness to be the practice of releasing our attachment to anything that locks up our creative energies. This is why forgiveness

---

[1] Margaret Visser, *Beyond Fate* (Toronto: House of Anansi Press, 2002), 44–46.

is a *life-orientation* and not only a discrete strategy for dealing with those who have hurt us.

Forgiveness, in this expanded definition, comes under the broader spiritual umbrella of releasing our attachment to anybody, any event, and any way of imagining reality that locks us into the past and keeps us in the realm of fate. For example, forgiveness is letting go of a self-image, or an image we have of another person, that freezes potential for spiritual evolution.

This is a more subtle practice of forgiveness in the service of a better, more wholesome future. For example, as an athlete in high school, I had a reputation of being the set-up man. I set up the star players and took a certain amount of pleasure in taking the back seat. I liked the role. It gave me a certain kind of status—enough to make all-star teams—but relieved me of the pressure of having to be the front guy. The story I had of myself was: Bruce, the set-up guy. I remember, however, when that began to change. I started to like to shoot the ball. I wanted the ball in pressure situations. I learned to thrive under pressure. If I had remained attached to an early self-image, this other side of me never would have emerged. There was a whole other depth of potential that was under lock and key of my earlier self-image of the set-up guy.

Families can unwittingly lock us into roles and stories that we unconsciously take on and live out. He's the sensitive one. She's the selfish one. He's the artist. She's the serious one. He struggles with life. She's trouble. We have an instinctive reaction against being pigeon-holed as this or that, because our souls know that we have the capacity to transcend the stories we tell ourselves or the stories that others tell themselves about who we are. We want to be free, and when we lock someone into a category, we limit his freedom to realize new and deeper dimensions of his being. In evolutionary spirituality, we know that our selves are works in progress, or better yet, working *processes*—the evolutionary process showing up in, through, and as us.

This is why it's important to answer the question, "What's your story?" Whose story are you living out? What story of yourself, or of reality in general, have you chosen to bind yourself to? Stay loose with those stories—creating a little healthy distance between these stories and who we are becoming. Hold them lightly, with curiosity. Enjoy them, play with them, develop the plot, but don't attach yourself to them. And release your attachment to the stories you tell about other people, too, especially the people with whom you are intimate. We easily slip into the practice of telling the same old stories about the people we love. We freeze them into an image of the past (and then get bored with them!).

Releasing self-images and stories about who we imagine ourselves to be is how the self evolves. In the early stages of the evolution of the self, we need others to help us let go of earlier images of ourselves. We need parents, school systems, and work environments to hold us safely within a particular expression of self, and then when the time is right, to let us go—to release us from the that image or story—so that we can discover new dimensions of self. In my example, if I had a coach who refused to let me exercise my desire to score, my environment would have failed me. Failures to hold and release, hold and release, result in failures to realize our deepest potentials. In an evolutionary model, this is serious. Our deepest potentials, in the end, are in the greater service of the evolution of the universe.

At a certain point in our development, we assume responsibility for our own evolutionary culture. We can't always depend on others to release us from limiting self-images. We cultivate the environments that give us the best opportunities to grow. This includes our friendships, our intimate relationships, and our work environments. This is what church is meant to be—a habitat or culture that holds you and then releases you, and encourages you to realize new dimensions of your being that can be in service to this one Earth community. Church is meant to be a culture of forgiveness, comprised of forgivers—those who have learned not to define others by their wrongdoings—and also those who know the practice of not being held hostage to earlier stories and images of self that bind us to fate. Through the practice of forgiveness, church becomes a destiny culture.

When Jesus taught the disciples to pray, "forgive us our debts, as we also have forgiven our debtors," he was drawing on the spiritual truth that our debts bind us to whomever, or whatever, we are indebted to (Matthew 6:12). When we absolutely bind ourselves or others to a particular image, worldview, or a single way of interpreting reality, we incur a debt. We are in debt to that story or that image. Like any debt, it must be repaid. And the currency with which this debt must be repaid is our freedom—the freedom to allow a new expression of self to emerge and be in service of this glorious adventure of life.

When the artist Cézanne had set up the subject that he was painting, his final step was to tilt his head to one side to gain a new perspective. That came to be called "Cézanne's doubt." In order not to be in debt to his past perspective, he introduced doubt. Cézanne's debt was forgiven by Cézanne's doubt. He practised doubting his preferred perspective of reality so that a fresh perspective could emerge. The practice of forgiveness, under this larger umbrella of releasing our attachment to self-image, worldviews, and interpretations of reality, is analogous to Cézanne's doubt. Sometimes, all it takes is a slight tilt of the head in order to claim this glorious gift of freedom. God releases you from fate, to realize your destiny. Now release others as you have been released.

The Better Part

Luke 10:38–42, Colossians 1:15–28

Mary takes off her apron and says, "Screw it. I'm not peeling carrots in the kitchen while these guys get to sit at Jesus's feet and grow in wisdom." Martha is flabbergasted. She immediately goes to Jesus and demands that he order Mary back into the kitchen to help her. Instead, Jesus tells Martha that Mary had chosen "the better part" (Luke 10:42).

Typical postmodern sermons on Luke 10:38–42 spend most of the time affirming that somebody has to take care of the household chores. Maybe Martha and Mary could have worked it out so that sometimes one listened to Jesus and then the next time it was the other one's turn. That would only be fair. Most sermons on this topic spend more time affirming the importance of the Marthas around the church than with the behaviour that Jesus affirmed in Mary. After all, a congregation couldn't run without Martha serving the coffee and doing the behind-the-scenes work. All true.

One of the fundamental characteristics of the postmodern or sensitive worldview is that value judgments are deemed to be bad. Nothing can be more valuable than anything else. Certainly, no person can be seen as doing something better than anybody else, or making an inherently better decision than anybody else. We're all equal, just different. Jesus couldn't have meant what he said, because he may have hurt Martha's feelings—and then for two thousand years hurt the feelings of all those who imagined themselves more in the role of Martha than Mary. So, basically, a whole bunch of sermons have apologized on behalf of Jesus for his insensitive remark. Today, Martha could take him to the Human Rights Commission.

Well, Jesus said it. It is written. And we have to deal with it. So what on Earth is there left to say about this little story that hasn't already been said? First of all, Mary's behaviour is marvellous. Here's a woman—two thousand years ago, when patriarchy was at its height, and women know very well their role in society—who steps outside of her prescribed role. It's difficult for us to appreciate the radical edge of what Mary did because we're steeped in a post-1960s world. Women have been sidestepping patriarchy now for fifty years. But two thousand years ago, it would have taken great courage.

So maybe Jesus was affirming Mary's risk to follow her soul's calling at a time when there was no precedent for what she did. Mary was laying down a template for new possibilities for women. When she took off the apron and sat at Jesus's feet to enroll in the academy of Wisdom, she opened up a whole new future for women. Here, God was doing something new: through Jesus, S/he was validating Mary's choice. Without this validation, that door into the future never would have opened. Jesus and Mary conspired to bring forth this future. So radical was their conspiracy that it took another couple thousand years for Mary's choice to become the norm. And we're still another fifty years away from Mary's choice being available to the majority of women across the world.

Mary teaches us a core practice of evolutionary Christian spirituality—to situate ourselves at the edge of the emerging future and be willing to step into the new thing that God is doing. We do it as an act of service to humanity and in the spirit of the Christ. This practice is very different from the traditional Christian mandate to guard the old order, thus ensuring that the unchanging truth of Christianity is established in each new age. The task of evolutionary Christians is to spend time up in the watchtower, scouring the horizon for signs of the future, of God coming into our lives in the present.

This story, then, is not just for women. It's for women and men who recognize in Mary a core characteristic of being in Christ. She asked herself: What is my soul's desire in this moment? What is preventing me from taking this next step? What does it mean in my life for Wisdom to have its way with me? If I don't step into the future now, then when? What will I lose if I don't take this opportunity? Mary chose to make this her first priority—"the better part" of anything else her life was about.

This brings me to the passage from Colossians, and the words seem pretty strange:

> He is the image of the invisible God, the firstborn of all creation; for in him all things in heaven and on earth were created, things visible and invisible, whether thrones or dominions or rulers or powers—all things have been created through him and for him. He himself is before all things, and in him all things hold together. He is the head of the body, the church; he is the beginning, the firstborn from the dead, so that he might come to have first place in everything. (Colossians 1:15–18)

This is Paul, the academic Jew, reflecting on the deep meaning of Jesus's life. Paul embodied the consciousness of the Christ—the very Heart and Mind of God. This Wisdom was present in Jesus. Paul imagines that this Wisdom took form in Jesus as the power of creation itself. S/he holds all things together. S/he is the binding power of the cosmos. Christ is meant to be first in all things because S/he is the first principle of the universe.

This Presence, alive in Jesus and waiting to be aroused in Mary and in all of us, is what caused Mary to take off her apron. This creative power reached into Mary's soul and there was nothing—no social convention, no disapproving man, no whining sister, no family obligation—that was going to keep her soul from flying to this one, the one in whom the universe is held together and brings forth new futures. She felt her destiny calling in and through Jesus, the Christ incarnate. She chose "the better part." The one who is first in all things became first in Mary's life, and she was reconciled to life in God, as Paul puts it later in the Colossians passage.

In Christ, God was reconciling all things to Godself. The etymological roots of *reconcile* give us the meaning of the word: it means to make friendly again.[1] Christ makes us friendly again with God. Mary's soul just wanted to befriend God, because she was missing the friendship. And if that holy friendship meant breaking a few rules, then so be it. No more pea shucking. She gets herself into the living room of soul, to sit at the feet of Wisdom. Nothing could stop her, in Paul's words, from becoming "mature in Christ" (Colossians 1:28).

Let us reconcile with the Holy One and the Holy Oneness, and let nothing get in the way of us befriending Spirit.

---

[1] "Reconcile," Dictionary.com, *Online Etymology Dictionary*, accessed November 6, 2011, http://dictionary.reference.com/browse/reconcile.

Stuck with the Cross?

Luke 14:25–33, Philemon 1:1–21

Jesus should have attended a few web-marketing seminars. In the world of online marketing, if you're selling something—say, a writing course—you start with a pitch that goes something like: "Write a best-seller in 30 days! Click here and begin your writing career!" Then you're taken to a landing page and offered a free download of the *Top Ten Tips for Becoming a Best-Selling Author*. Easy. It's streamlined, and you can do it in your spare time, to boot. For the giveaway price of just $169, your dream can become your reality, today, with just one more click. With online marketing, you do not want to make it sound like whatever it is you're selling is going to be an ordeal to obtain.

Jesus, on the other hand, is trying to sell discipleship, and he ain't soft-pedalling the product. It's spiritual boot camp. And it's going to be tough! First, you need to hate your family—nay, "even life itself,"—if you are interested in signing up (Luke 14:26). Clearly this is a niche market. He goes on to say that you have to be willing to carry the cross to be his disciple. Whoopee, that sounds like fun. Who wants to sign up? His message is clear and blunt. Just as a king has to clearly calculate the costs and benefits of going to war, anybody who intends to follow Jesus should carefully consider the options. An internet-marketing coach wouldn't know where to start with a client like Jesus.

I'm no marketer, but I am charged with the task of articulating why on Earth anyone would want to take up the Christian life. And here,

Jesus is clearly not helping his own cause, at least not by contemporary public relations standards.

The cross is central in Luke 14:25–33 and in the church, for that matter, and it is a tough sell—especially in today's spiritual marketplace. There was a time when religion was pretty much the same fare for everyone in a society. But today, religion is a buffet, not a fixed menu. It consists of dollops of this and that. We are free to choose only the dishes we like, and leave the rest. This may be a good thing. But it does leave us with a dilemma. At the smorgasbord of religious symbols, people choose almost any symbol over a cross. Why a cross when you can have a crystal, an astrological chart, a medicine wheel, a mantra, or a mandala? Our symbol is decidedly out of fashion.

Reverend Ian Lawton and his United Church of Christ congregation in the U.S. decided to remove the cross from their church building. They changed their name to C3 Exchange, eliminating any reference to Christ or to church. Fox News picked up on the cross removal, and Ian received a lot of email, some of which bordered on hate mail. In the so-called "progressive" church, the cross is a conundrum. We don't know whether to remove it, ignore it, or soft-pedal it. For a great many spiritual seekers, it is simply a nonstarter, and sermons referencing the cross make many look around for the nearest exit.

The congregation I serve at Canadian Memorial United Church has a particular problem: a stained-glass window with the crucified Jesus towering over us. We are not going to remove the window, but it makes the option of ignoring it very difficult. It's actually strange in a Protestant church to have an image of Jesus hanging from the cross. Usually, that image is found only in Roman Catholic churches. We could soft-pedal it—say, devote one sermon to it per year on Good Friday but otherwise just treat the window as little more than pretty coloured glass.

However, the cross issue has recently been the source of some behind-the-scenes discernment at Canadian Memorial. We have a great website, but because we're always asking ourselves what our next evolutionary step is, we're redesigning the site to give us increased flexibility and capacity. We asked a graphic designer to create a new logo. The first one had a very subtle image of the cross, the kind of image that emerges after a few seconds of staring at it—like those 3-D images that eventually present themselves once you acquire a soft focus. When we took it out for a test drive, we discovered that those who had been associated with church for some time had no problem with the cross, but spiritual seekers with less church background had a strong negative reaction to it.

Here's what happens when they see the cross: They think of Mel Gibson and *The Passion of the Christ*. They associate it with the theology that says that the more Jesus suffers on the cross, the more God must love us. Even without a lifetime of being taught that this somehow makes sense, they are repulsed.

Our evangelical and fundamentalist friends have cornered the market on the cross. It's strange that the cross has been hijacked by atonement theology—Christ dying for our sins, and salvation by believing the right things—because the theology is actually very complex and, to my mind, convoluted.

So are we *stuck* with the cross, then? Well, I'd rather change the frame. Not surprisingly, I have an idea for a frame that we might use—an evolutionary one! The truth is that there is no single meaning of the cross, and it never had a single meaning in this history of Christianity. Even within the New Testament, you have many interpretive lenses. Here's what happened: Jesus was crucified. The first followers were left with the task of interpreting the meaning of a good man, a God-man, being executed by the state. So they wrote about it from within the context of their own worldview and life situation. And we're still trying to make sense of it. In two thousand years, we'll still be trying to make sense of it.

The meanings that emerge reflect the consciousness and the culture of the meaning-maker. Different worldviews bring forth different interpretations. Each is true, from that worldview, but partial.

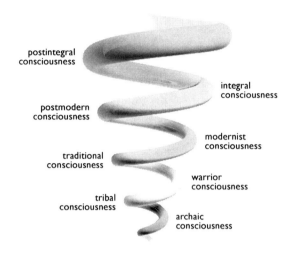

postintegral consciousness

integral consciousness

postmodern consciousness

modernist consciousness

traditional consciousness

warrior consciousness

tribal consciousness

archaic consciousness

Spiral dynamic worldviews. Reproduced from *Integral Consciousness and the Future of Evolution* by Steve McIntosh; used by permission.

At a tribal worldview, the cross is viewed through a magical consciousness. Here, the cross might act as a kind of magical amulet to ward off evil spirits. This might be what the cross is used for in voodoo religion, for example. Here, a person might wear a cross to protect himself against evil spells.

A warrior worldview associates the cross with victory. My god can trounce your god. Notice that when athletes go down on one knee and cross themselves after a match or a game, they do so only after a win—never a loss. They kiss their cross, often times, because their god has triumphed over the enemy. The theology is that somehow God *triumphed* on the cross (even though it looked like God took a loss).

In a traditional worldview, God has a foreordained, divine plan for the world, and the cross is just part of God's plan for salvation. Jesus had to die to save human beings from sin, and if you believe it, then you are saved. Jesus necessarily died on the cross for the divine plan to be carried out. This is still the dominant association with the cross across the planet.

With the arrival of the modern worldview, reason predominates. We question the rational basis for our beliefs. Science plays the important role of demythologizing religious beliefs. For example, Stephen Hawking has declared that the universe doesn't need God. And he gives a thoroughly rationalist argument.[1] In this worldview, Jesus becomes, in Dom Crossan's phrase, "a Jewish peasant with an attitude"[2]—not the divine Son of God. The cross, stripped of its theological and metaphysical meanings, becomes merely an effective instrument of state torture. It was Rome's best means of crowd control. Few who witnessed a crucifixion had appetite for rebellion.

Approximately fifty years ago, with the war in Vietnam and the women's liberation movement, the limits of reason became apparent to the human species en masse. The modernist emphasis on individual freedom, unconstrained by religion or an overseer God, had rendered more than two-thirds of the world's population to the status of left-behinds. A sensitive or *empathic* consciousness emerged in postmodernism. The cross became a symbol of God's solidarity with all of the victims of society. God's response to human suffering was to suffer with us—in Jesus on the cross. (This interpretation of the cross is the go-to interpretation of the United Church of Canada.) Or again, from this worldview, the cross is a symbol of how God, in Jesus, transforms the violence of humanity into God's own suffering on the cross rather than perpetuate the cycle of retaliation.

And today, there is an emerging worldview that some call integral. In this stage, we are able to affirm rather than trash the other

---

[1] Stephen Hawking and Leonard Mlodinow, *The Grand Design* (New York: Bantam Books, 2010).

[2] John Dominic Crossan, *The Birth of Christianity: Discovering What Happened in the Years Immediately After the Execution of Jesus* (New York: HarperCollins Publishers, 1998), xxx.

worldviews' interpretations of reality. It is integrative, rather than dismissive. We see both the dignity and downside of every worldview and interpretation of reality. And we allow new interpretations to emerge.

Integral consciousness understands the cross as a symbol or a metaphor of transformation. The cross and resurrection describe a process that we all go through as we spiritually mature. Spiritual evolution requires us to "die with Christ" in terms of worldviews, beliefs, and values that are no longer complex enough to make sense of our lives. This is very painful, as anyone who has transitioned from one worldview to another can testify. It feels like a death of the soul.

The emergence of a new worldview is a type of resurrection. It's not the end of the world, but rather the beginning of a new one. This process never ends. This is what Jesus means when he says that we must hate life itself. Metaphorically, this means that you should never become so attached to your life as it is—to your assumptions about reality, your beliefs, or the stories that you tell yourself about your life and life itself—that you cannot let this life go when the time comes. You must always be prepared to allow these worldviews to die—to be crucified—when the time is right. This is what it means to carry the cross. It's an orientation in life. Carrying our cross means learning the delicate art of dying, again and again, as a strategy for spiritual evolution—and in preparation for our physical death, so that we may die well.

The story of Onesimus, the slave, and Philemon, the slave's owner, is an example of Paul exhorting a new Christian (Philemon) to carry the cross and hate his life—metaphorically speaking. In the new age of Christ, it was clear to Paul that slavery was out. (Empires, including the Roman Empire, were built upon the foundation of slavery. It was only 150 years ago or so that anybody began to seriously question slavery in the way that Paul did two thousand years ago.) To be in Christ was to be crucified to this institution, in Paul's opinion. Onesimus was already a free man in the age of Christ consciousness, and Philemon needed to die to the social norms, the economic system, and unconscious assumptions that told him that slavery was an acceptable institution in God's eyes. Philemon needed to undergo a profound transformation of consciousness—a metaphorical crucifixion. He may not have sat down and counted the cost when he "put on" Christ (Romans 13:14).

We're not "stuck" with the cross. Rather, we're entrusted with it. You walk into a church and the cross signals that death is waiting for all of us—you might as well deal with it now, rather than wait until the moment of your last breath. Sure, the world might want to turn away from it; the world has wanted to turn away from the cross right from the start. It was foolishness to the Greek philosophers, and it is blasphemous for our contemporary society that equates the good life with a happy face. To turn away from it, though, is to walk away from the mystery that lies on the other side of death. It is to walk away from what Spirit is inviting you to bring into the world when you walk through that frightening portal. To walk away from the cross and the death that it brings is, paradoxically, to walk away from life, in the form of all the unrealized potential that can only be realized by risking death and discovering what is on the other side.

We are not told if Philemon freed his slave Onesimus. But I like to imagine that he did. I like to imagine that he carried his cross and faced whatever it was inside of him, inside of society, and inside of his culture that needed to die. Because on the other side of his terrible and wondrous letting go, there is a resurrection—a resurrection named abolition, and the freedom that it brought to slaves and slave owners alike. I like to think that he carried the cross, and by doing so, Philemon was a spiritual pioneer, laying down a template for freedom that would take another two thousand years for our species to realize—but could have never happened if somebody hadn't been the first to go to the cross.

So, no, Jesus won't win any marketing awards. And the cross is here to stay, thank God. This pattern of living, this death and resurrection that never ends, leads us into the very Heart of Spirit. To walk this path and carry the cross is to be in Spirit every step of the journey. What is on offer is the abundant life of Christ. So let's die together and discover the life that awaits us on the other side of death.

Conversation That Evolves

Mark 12:28-34

A scribe overhears a crowd "disputing" and notices that Jesus is more than holding his own. He enters the fray himself. Here, my mind lingers on the significance of the theological discussion the community was having, likely facilitated by Jesus. I'm not so interested in *what* they were talking about, but rather *that* they were having a theological discussion. Didn't they have anything better to do? There must have been some cause somewhere that they could have been supporting. Why stand around and talk about God when there was so much to do?

I know the text says they were disputing, but when Jews get together to have a theological discussion, it can sound more like a dispute than a conversation. But it's not necessarily an argument. Jewish libraries in the first century were not like libraries today. They buzzed with lively conversation about one point of the Law or another. It was part of the culture. They gathered together to talk about God and the nature of ultimate reality.

I love this, because theological (or spiritual) conversation needs to regain a central place in the life of a spiritual community. We need to be talking about God with each other. I suspect that we are in an era when people are afraid of wading into these kinds of conversations for fear of being wrong or unorthodox, as though there are right answers to theological questions. But, I'll let you in on a little secret: nobody knows the answers. No minister, pope, theology professor, or saint has the correct answer to the question of God. You can't get it wrong!

Having said that, there are more and less thoughtful ways to be in conversation. In our culture, religion is one of the big three taboo dinner table conversation topics. This taboo was instituted because we have lost the art of holy conversation. Our little selves get talking about religion, and right away we want to make a point, *our* point. We've read a thing or two about this, and we're pretty sure we're right on the point. So you end up with winners and losers, and an arrogant person who feels like he's won, while the rest of the guests go home thinking that guy was an idiot.

It takes practice to be in this kind of conversation, and one of the church's roles is to create forums for you to practise. Our culture has become obsessively pragmatic. If it's not "useful," why bother? Our politicians want to turn the education system into a factory for future contributors to the economic system. But we might think about education as an extended conversation between students and teachers that becomes increasingly sophisticated over the years. The education system becomes the forum in which students learn the rules of engagement.

The ancient Greeks may have been the first culture to realize the sacred nature of this kind of conversation, which they called philosophy. Socrates developed what became known, not surprisingly, as Socratic dialogue. He discovered that reasoned conversation taken to its extreme was actually a way of tapping into a sacred dimension, the mind of God. Our capacity for reason was our own little divine spark. One of his students, Plato, developed this system of rational discourse even further. But please don't confuse what Socrates and Plato were about with "talk, talk, talk. . ." They developed philosophical communities, and the lives of people in those communities were daily, disciplined applications of reason. Philosophy, for them, was applied reason. It wasn't abstract, like it can be today. Conversation was both an end in itself and the means by which you discovered how to live a sacred and virtuous life.

These philosophical conversations were not about developing a comprehensive system of knowledge, with the goal of knowing everything you could possibly know about reality. They developed rigorous techniques of helping people take conversations to the very limits of reason, where they discovered that what they *didn't* know was much greater than what they did know. Put another way, they discovered what they *thought* they knew was an arbitrary construction. This liberated them from pre-existing, cultural assumptions, which students unconsciously turned into fixed ideas, beliefs, and values. By discovering what they didn't know, they were able to open up to broader, more encompassing and nuanced ideas, beliefs, and values.

One disciple of Socrates described walking around in a stupor for weeks on end after a three-day conversation with his teacher. He was in a state of aporia—profound doubt—about the meaning he had made of life. He was, to use a phrase from our mystical tradition, in a "cloud of unknowing." This cloud of unknowing would eventually lead him to live his life in a radically different way than when he had attained certainty. By loosening his attachment to his own belief system, he was able to consciously participate in the evolution of his consciousness. In other words, the goal of reasoned conversation was to lead the participants away from certainty and toward the emergence of new wisdom. Doubt was the philosopher's ally.

This has always been the goal of theological conversation as well. We press each other to the very limits of our definitions and interpretations of God—not so that we can ultimately define God, but rather to help us realize that all of our definitions of God fall short. God is ineffable mystery. And where the human community gets into trouble is when somebody or some community comes along with an absolute, definitive understanding of God. When you come across this, run, don't walk, in the other direction.

The film *Being There*, with Peter Sellers playing Chauncey Gardiner, caused me to doubt the entire foundation of my faith system.

Chauncey is a simpleton gardener who says things like, "First comes spring and summer, but then we have fall and winter. And then we get spring and summer again," and people become convinced that he is a spiritual master. At a time when my own conservative faith structure was breaking down, this story acted like a wrecking ball. It caused me to fear that Jesus was really a naive Galilean peasant, not a Saviour figure. I was profoundly disoriented. Sacred conversation can do the same thing. It may cause us to suspend our tidy little stories about God. That's why Jesus told parables. Parables are a literary genre designed to subvert conventional myths. They sneak inside those conventional myths with a story that everybody can relate to, and then the bomb goes off, and everything you thought you knew is shaken to the core. This kind of rigorous discourse is not always pleasant, but it is a way to evolve.

In the ninth century, Denys the Areopagite developed a method of theological conversation intended to bring the participants to a state of contemplative silence, when all that can be said has been said, and all that remains is to rest in the omnipresence of the One who cannot be described in words. But Denys, too, had rules of engagement. First, you define God. You say, "God is like a rock." God is solid, supportive, the ground beneath our feet. Then you talk about how ridiculous this metaphor actually is: God is obviously not like a rock. A rock is inanimate, uncaring, and incapable of goodness. Next, you deny that you can even say anything about what God is not like: you can't even say that God is not like a rock, because God is so far beyond our limited capacity. Then you fall into silence, and know the unknowable One through direct experience. First affirm, then deny, then deny the denial, then rest in the presence of the unknowable One.

The paradox is that we participate in reasoned conversation about God knowing that we'll never know and, what's more interesting, knowing that the very impulse to engage in this conversation, and the reasoning we bring to the conversation, comes from the unknowable God.

Through reasoned conversation that will leave us in a cloud of unknowing, we experience the unknowable One at the limits of reason! Now, that's good conversation.

The conversation in Mark's gospel turns to the greatest commandment: Hear, O Israel, the Lord, your God, is One, and we are to love God with all our heart and soul and mind and strength, and our neighbour as ourselves.

In Hebrew, the word for "one" is *echadh*. The mystical tradition of Judaism, the Kabala, interprets this word to mean that God is Oneness, the divine essence present in all of creation—unknowable in essence, yet present in every part. Each part, even a leaf blowing in the wind, is a reflection of this divine Oneness. When we are able to see God in everything and everybody, we respond with awe and love. We love God. We love the other as ourselves, because beneath, within, above, and below our differences, we are expressions of the One God. What we have in common is original. The ways in which we differ are secondary to this fundamental unity. Our neighbour is an occasion of divine presence, as are we, so we love our neighbour as ourselves. And then we reorient and reorient and reorient our lives around this hidden, unknowable Oneness; this unity is the most real thing about life.

Imagine beginning our conversations with the awareness that this sacred unity is present in and *as* our conversation partners. If so, we would confer deep respect and honour in the way we listen, in the words we choose to speak, and how we choose to show up for the conversation. We would assume that this divine manifestation has wisdom for us. What we would *not* do is show up with our tautologies or yesterday's wisdom.

The end goal of these conversations is to create a habitat for the emergence of sacred Wisdom, who makes all things new. By deeply attending to one another's wisdom, and allowing this temporary articulation to be deepened and advanced, truth would evolve through the conversation. We would not offer our tried and true conclusions about life, but rather the fresh truth that comes from the edges of our consciousness—truth that we may not have had time to absolutely nail down but that comes forward through the flow of the conversation. We would learn to be so attuned to Spirit that if something were offered that felt like it were coming from the little self, we would know it. You can feel this when it works. It's like Wisdom is connecting more deeply with itself—or not. "Truth" emerges in and through a collective dynamic, not residing in any single person. This is the kind of evolutionary conversation I want to be involved in.

Wings for the Weary

Mark 1:29-39

At night, Deepak Chopra falls into a sleep-and-meditation pattern: he sleeps for thirty minutes, then meditates for thirty minutes, then sleeps for thirty more minutes, and meditates again for another thirty minutes. He gets up at 4:00 a.m. and meditates for another two hours. He sleeps for maybe a few hours per night. In the morning, his secretary tells him where he's supposed to be and what he'll be doing there.[1] This author of more than fifty books travels the world, gives lectures, offers workshops, and keeps a schedule that would exhaust most mortals. How does he do it?

Not long ago, I co-led a workshop with Barbara Marx Hubbard in Chicago. At the time of writing, Barbara is eighty-two. She's about to launch a TV show. She already has a radio show. This past year, she trained thousands of people to be Agents of Conscious Evolution. After the workshop in Chicago, she flew back to her home in Santa Barbara, California, packed another suitcase, and left the next morning to lead another workshop. What amazes people who experience Barbara is her seemingly inexhaustible energy supply. She shows no signs of slowing down.

Jesus kept a pretty amazing schedule himself. Mark 1:29–39 depicts him healing Peter's mother-in-law of a fever. The crowds are lined

---

[1] Andrew Cohen, "The Mythic Life and Times of Deepak Chopra," *EnlightenNext magazine*, May–July 2008, http://www.enlightennext.org/magazine/j40/chopra.asp?.

up outside the door, waiting for their own healing. Jesus sneaks out before dawn to find a quiet place. The disciples find him and tell him that the crowds are waiting for him to return. But he's ready to move on to other villages to continue his healing work. His schedule would have also exhausted most people, and yet we hear him in another passage calling all of those who are weary and laden with burdens to come to *him*. He would offer *them* rest. How did he do it?

The author of Isaiah contrasts mere mortals, even youth in the high-energy phase of life, with God, the Source and Font of all energy: "Even youths will faint and be weary, and the young will fall exhausted" (Isaiah 40:30), but God, "He does not faint or grow weary" (40:28). God is the Source of all energy, who continually pours out energy without exhausting the supplies: God the Supplier. So what do modern mystics like Deepak Chopra and Barbara Marx Hubbard, and ancient prophets like Jesus know, that keeps them going? Deepak Chopra has a disciplined meditation practice. Barbara spends time every day tapping into the Creative Process of the Universe itself. Jesus was forever stealing away to a quiet place to drop back into the Source he called the Father. They each have a direct supply line to the Source, and in truth, each of them imagines themselves to be a divine manifestation in human form. Don't worry, they would tell you that you are as well!

Yet it's not their energy, per se, that interests me. It's what this conscious dropping into divinity makes of the energy. By tapping into a deeper source, their energy is sanctified and focused in service of a higher, sacred purpose. That higher purpose is differently defined by each of them. For Jesus, it was the realization of the Kin(g)dom of God on Earth. A big part of the challenge for our fledgling species is that we haven't collectively awakened to what it is we're meant to use our energy for. Despite living through the most affluent period of civilization, citizens of Western democracies continue to use their energy in the service of mere survival and for displays of status, as though we still lived in a jungle. We exhaust ourselves playing the money game, chasing after the next big thing, converting natural, social, and spiritual capital into money—because money masquerades as a god.

But money is not a source of energy. In fact, we have to spend life energy and natural capital in order to get it. Most of us are exhausting ourselves, and inadvertently exhausting our planet's resources, spending our true capital—life energy—on that which does not renew. So if we're going to break our unconscious confusion of money with a god, we had better be clear what our life energy is for. Our species is the "youth" that Isaiah is describing, growing faint, weary, and exhausted in our relentless chasing after money.

But God does not grow weary. And those who wait upon the Lord do not grow weary, because they are in service to a purpose beyond mere survival. But how do you wait upon the Lord? What exactly does that mean? It doesn't mean waiting for an external God to do something that we can't do ourselves. It means to consciously align with, identify with, and be nourished by the sacred Source of all energy. In doing so, we not only gain energy for survival, we gain energy for serving a divine purpose. And when we do this, our soul awakens because it finally has something to do that matters.

I want to suggest three fundamental pathways to this eternal Font of energy. The first is to spend time cultivating awe. Be in nature. Watch documentaries. Learn the story of the universe. Study science. Do whatever it takes for you to get stopped in your tracks by the sheer beauty, complexity, and intelligence that is coursing through life on our planet. Our policy makers and our politicians should drop into the fragile beauty and intricacy of our ecosystems. We as a species should appreciate, in the words of the psalmist, how we are "fearfully and wonderfully made" (Psalm 139:14). Whoever penned the words to that psalm wrote without the benefit of science. He couldn't have had any idea as to how elegant the human body truly is. He couldn't have known how the adaptive striving and intelligence of all the creatures that preceded us on this planet forged our bodies. He couldn't have known that we are the universe's resumé, in human form. If we are not familiar with the condition of awe, we have no business writing environmental policy. If we are not able to bow before beauty and elegance, we will inevitably end up serving the interests of money, because the ego serves only security, and money is security's god.

But those who are able to fall silent before the sheer miracle of life will connect with the energy that is coursing through all life forms. And once you have genuinely connected with this pulsing energy, you will want to harness that power for the good of all creation. The Lord shall renew your strength; you shall mount up with wings like eagles; you shall run and not be weary; you shall walk and not faint.

The second pathway that gives wings to the weary is to find your heart. Do whatever you need to do—first to find, and then to soften, your heart. Waiting for the Lord means orienting from your heart center. It requires a commitment to feel what's in your heart before acting, speaking, or committing to anything. Find your heart, and allow it to melt and flow like warm lava. Hang out with people who love you unconditionally, and love them back in relationships of reciprocity that build the field of love. Find a community of love, comprised of those who have arrived at a point in their lives when they've tried everything else and have come to realize that it pretty much comes down to love. Connect with love and you will connect with the power that gave birth to our universe.

The heart center is located midway along the line of energy centers (chakras) in our body. This is where the energies of Earth and the transcendent spiritual energies meet. If, as a species, we're making decisions without connecting to our hearts, they will be bad decisions. If we are creating new technology from hardened hearts, that technology will not be in service of life. It will be in service of money. But if our best minds are connected to our hearts, then our technology can serve the future of our planet and life itself. The new human, Homo sapiens sapiens 2.0—doctors, lawyers, trade workers, clergy, scientists, inventors, engineers, politicians, and philosophers—are rooted in heart intelligence. Those who live from their hearts shall renew their strength; they shall mount up with wings like eagles; they shall run and not be weary; they shall walk and not faint. They will be in service to love, and nothing bad ever came of love.

The third pathway to eternal life—by which I mean access to the self-renewing divine energy at the heart of life—is to find practices that help you overcome the illusion of separation. For the past three hundred years, we as a species have been making decisions based in a belief in fundamental disconnection: of humans from Earth; of the divine from the human; of men from women; of heads from hearts; of matter from spirit; of Earth from a living, learning universe; of science and technology from spiritual wisdom; of economics from ecology; of body from soul; of the socially privileged from the cast-offs. This list is endless. It is endless because the illusion of separation has turned difference into disconnection, and from disconnection into dissociation. Dissociation is a state of spiritual and psychological autism.

The greatest spiritual masters of history and of our age share this in common: they know that Reality is One. Everything and everybody are fruit of the single tree of life. We come from the same Source; we are that Source wearing a human body; we are nourished by that Source; we will return to that Source, and then we'll assume a new form and a new consciousness. It's a great recycling program, with Spirit taking "endless forms most beautiful and most wonderful" (to use Darwin's phrase for diversity).[2]

Sufi poet, Hafiz, intuited Spirit's recycling program, this single, sacred energy, this one tree of life bearing much fruit.

---

[2] Charles Darwin, *On the Origin of Species by Means of Natural Selection* (New York: D. Appleton and Company, 1870), 425.

Look! I Am a Whale[3]

We live on the Sun's playground.

Here,
Everyone get's what they want.

Sometimes the body of a beautiful woman,
Sometimes the body of a beautiful man,
Sometimes the body of both
In one.

We used to play that kind of tag
In the animal world too.

Now a mouse,
Now a tiger,
Look! I am a whale—I got tired of the land,
Went back to the ocean for a while.

What power is it in our sinew and mind
That will not die,

That keeps us shopping for the perfect dress?

We have all heard the Flute Player
And keep dancing
Toward Him.

Hafiz,
You have seen the Flute Player
And cannot help but
Whirl.

---

[3] Hafiz, "Look! I Am a Whale" *The Gift: Poems by Hafiz, the Great Sufi Master,* trans. Daniel Ladinsky (Toronto: Penguin Group, 1999), 122.

Note how in the middle of this poem, Hafiz asks the question, "What power is it in our sinew and mind / That will not die, // That keeps shopping for the perfect dress?" "Perfect dress" is his metaphor for diversity.

What is this power within us, and within all, that will not die? Some call it God. Some call it Spirit. Others call it Mystery, or Life. It really doesn't matter what we call it, but it does matter that we learn to dance while listening to its music. It does matter that we learn to identify with this energy that will not die—at least for the time we have on this extraordinary planet.

This is what all the great spiritual masters have discovered—they are the splendid dress that Spirit has chosen to wear for this brief sojourn through life on Earth, and when they dance, they dance with the energy and eternal vitality of Spirit. And when the dance is over, they know that they will return to that which will not die. There is no disconnection anywhere, just different forms and unique expressions of one Spirit, calling us to awaken and become the best expression we can be of the Oneness-in-diversity.

Drop into awe, open your heart, and awaken into Oneness. Be in service in your own radiant and unique way to this one blessed universe. This doesn't take a lifetime of spiritual practice. Spiritual practice is just a response to the always, already present wonder, love, and unity of this blessed power that gives wings to the weary and strength to the faint. Let us mount up and soar into a new future for humanity, which is coming through us.

The New Deal for the Old Church

Luke 13:6-9

The owner of the vineyard was ready to cut down the fig tree. It was a waste of space. The fruit tree wasn't bearing fruit, which was its purpose, after all. Why keep it? A fruitless tree in the Bible is code for God's people. Bearing fruit is a condition of our covenant with God. The owner, according to the parable, has had enough. "Cut it down!" he tells the gardener.

We have a lovely tree on our front lawn that produces beautiful orange berries in the fall. But our neighbours have been doing extensive landscaping for the last couple of years, and the tree is showing serious signs of distress. This fall, there was only half the usual number of berries. Our gardener suggested doing radical root surgery—to the tune of $800! When I heard the cost, the words that formed in my consciousness were the owner's words: *Cut it down*.

Whether this is the voice of God or an inner voice of withering judgment is an open question. But we are all familiar with it, are we not? We make a mistake—screw up in some way—and a voice of condemnation sounds in our head, "Cut it down." We tell ourselves, "You are a waste of space." We tend to listen to this voice. Perhaps we first heard it from a parent, who themselves heard it from their parents. It's passed down the generations, and, eventually, we don't need anybody else telling us. It becomes our inner voice. It's the cause of a lot of misery in our lives and in society. We somehow got the idea that anything less than perfect is unacceptable, and when we don't attain it, we hear this voice: "Cut it down."

We hear this voice as a church, coming at us from society. I received an email the other day from a woman who had mistakenly got on our email list. She told me in no uncertain terms that (a) she wanted to unsubscribe, and (b) the church was evil. She was a practising Wiccan, a nature-based spirituality. The church had burned her sisters at the stake, she told me. She signed off with two words, the first word began with an *f* and the second word ended with two more *f*s. Not only has the church not born fruit in her mind, it had been an agent of death. "Cut it down," she was saying.

One or two of our church neighbours share the same sentiment. We do quite a few weddings at Canadian Memorial, and some of the neighbours aren't happy when the Saturday wedding traffic robs them of their street parking. They don't get "church" and could do quite well without it. One gentleman threatened to take us to court. We live in an age when to live across from a church is an annoyance. "Cut it down."

Secular culture just doesn't get church. The modernist period was characterized by a rallying cry that boiled down to cut it down. Who needs superstition? Who needs priests telling us to believe what science is revealing to be a chimera? Who needs a Bible written from a premodern consciousness that sometimes advocates violence, that is filled with strange codes of behaviour, and that often portrays God as a judge and executioner? Even today, muscular atheists, such as scientist Richard Dawkins and journalist Christopher Hitchens, reflect an early enlightenment mindset by claiming that rationalism and science have simply elbowed out the need for religion of any kind.[1] They are very vocal and active in their agenda to cut it down.

Well, these voices can get to you if you happen to be the fig tree. And, honestly, who hasn't felt as though it's time to cut simply cut it

---

[1] See Richard Dawkins, *The God Delusion* (Boston: Houghton Mifflin Harcourt, 2006), and Christopher Hitchens, *God Is Not Great: How Religion Poisons Everything* (Toronto: McClelland and Stewart, 2007).

down? I've spoken at churches around the country—and the situation isn't pretty. The Reverend David Ewart produced a nifty YouTube video showing graphically all the stats, and if the current trends continue, the United Church will reach the point of no return by 2030 at the latest.[2] The tree is stressed, the leaves are dropping, and the fruit is certainly sparse. Maybe, the season of the church has come to an end. Maybe it is time to cut it down.

But then another voice, rather forceful, in fact, surfaces: "Leave it alone for one more year. I'll dig around it, put some manure on it. Then, let's see what happens. If it bears fruit, great. If it doesn't, then fine, you can cut it down." It's a realistic voice, wouldn't you say? There are still conditions. The tree must bear fruit—after all, it's a fruit tree. But it's a voice of hope. A second chance is being offered. This surprising and unexpected voice is an advocate, not an adversary. This voice is saying that if we spend time getting down to the roots of the problem, if we give it nourishment, if we create the proper conditions, then maybe the tree can flourish. Maybe there's nothing wrong with the fig tree. Maybe, just maybe, it just needs the right kind of support.

Notice the authority in this voice. The gardener actually confronts the owner. "Leave it alone!" He's not asking. He's advocating: "I know a thing or two about helping things to grow and flourish." Notice, as well, the gardener does more than hope. He's willing to back up the hope by getting his hands dirty.

I've spend a lot of time with United Church gardeners across Canada. These are leaders of the church, both clergy and lay people who aren't prepared to concede that the fig tree called "church" is finished quite yet. But here's a paradox when it comes to church: They find that their worst enemy is not the voice of the public, and it's not modernist atheists. Often, it's the congregation itself. On the one hand, these good people of the congregation *sound* like the gardener:

---

[2] "The United Church at 100 in 2 Minutes and 25 Seconds – Revised,"YouTube video; 4:18, posted by davidewart1945, May 7, 2009, http://www.youtube.com/watch?v=BF4LMiqc370.

"*Don't* cut down the tree." In fact, they want their leaders to save the tree. But it can't be the voice of the gardener because, on the other hand, they are saying: "Just don't go digging around the roots. Don't add any manure. Don't introduce any changes. Just leave the church alone. Let's keep doing what we've always done, and hope that the tree magically starts to bear fruit."

But in the parable, that's not the deal. The deal is let's try some root surgery on this tree, and if it doesn't bear fruit, then it gets cut down. The fig tree *is* withering. It's one or the other—remove it or help it produce fruit. Notice that the owner is not even prepared to preside over a slow death. He's not saying: "Poor thing. We'll have to just let it sit there, for years and years, until the last drop of life has gone out of this pathetic excuse for a tree." And the gardener isn't exactly sentimental either. He's prepared to go to work and support the life that is remaining to see if it can rejuvenate the whole tree. But he's not prepared to preside over a protracted death.

You can perhaps see the analogy with our beloved United Church of Canada. We're called to bear fruit. That's our reason for existence as God's people. And we're in a season of repair. The voice of Christ, our advocate gardener, is on our side. But he's recommending tree surgery. And you need a diagnosis of the problem before you start digging around. Here's my diagnosis:

We have a sap problem. The energy is not flowing. It's getting stuck somewhere. My own theology is evolutionary in nature. God is *in* the evolutionary process of growth, and evolutionary growth is in God. Ever notice how many parables, just like this story, are about growth? From the womb of God emerged an evolutionary universe. But we're stuck. And we're stuck at a particular worldview in the United Church called postmodernism—featuring the "sensitive self." This worldview gave us many good things—pluralism, egalitarianism, a consensus-seeking bias, social justice, and the group hug! All good things—but its shadow side is killing us.

We're hard on our leaders. Our fear of hierarchy is so deep that we find ways to flatten the excellent in our midst. We confuse dominator hierarchies, which do need to be constructed, with natural hierarchies, which are the way the universe evolves. Our seminaries should have entire departments dedicated to teaching leadership. There's a reason we don't. It represents an unconscious, postmodernist bias. Everybody must be equal in every way. Nobody can shine. We have subtle, and not-so-subtle, ways of keeping our leaders in check—at all levels of the church, including in our congregations. The early church believed that we each had particular gifts, from the Spirit, and the key to healthy communities was helping people find their genius and letting people serve from their spiritual gifts. Let's let our leaders lead. Let's celebrate them rather than find subtle and not-so-subtle ways to bring them down a notch.

Postmodernism gave us many gifts, including the insight that all truth arises in and through context and perspective. But some postmodernists took this one step further—the nihilistic assumption that there is no truth in the universe except the arbitrary meaning that we construct. When all is context and perspective, truth disappears, and when truth goes, conviction goes along with it. When we lose our conviction as a church, the sap stops running and the tree will soon die. By conviction I mean a deep and abiding confidence that God has called us and equipped us to realize the Kin(g)dom of God in our place and time. You don't have to be a biblical literalist or a narrow-minded fundamentalist to experience this kind of conviction. Originally, the word *belief* had less to do with intellectual assent to a bunch of doctrines, and more to do with a heart-felt conviction that Spirit is enabling you and I to shape a new future.

Finally, we need to stop hurting each other. Our congregations are a mess across Canada because we are living out the hellish dramas of personal egos that have not gone to the wilderness and done the work that Jesus did before he started his ministry. The temptation story of Jesus is the ancient, mythological equivalent of what today would be called shadow work. Our personal and collective shadows are killing us as communities of faith. We haven't helped our people through the spiritual practice of getting to the root of all our unresolved personal dramas. Yes, I'm advocating therapy, spiritual direction, coaching—whatever it takes—to get our beloved church to deal with unresolved anger, sexual repression, inability to be self-defined, and to be able to communicate directly and compassionately from our most vulnerable selves. As a church, we passed right by the gift of modernity, which is the capacity to transcend, through conscious awareness, the personal dramas that our little selves love so much. We are hurting each other in our congregations, and as long as we continue to do so, all of our sap will go into perpetuating and then dealing with dramas that have nothing to do with revealing and realizing the Kin(g)dom of God.

What will help to get the sap flowing? Creative self-expression is the sap of life. We need a theology that helps people realize and feel the immense creativity that flows through them. We're still living on the fumes of a redemption-based theology that is not in touch with reality as we know it to be—as science has revealed it to be. Namely, the universe is evolving. It's evolving through you and through us. God is within this irrepressible impulse. We are the presence of that impulse, after 13.7 billion years, in personal form. The same creativity that brought forth a universe is now flowing through you and me.

We have this immense creative power within us that is Spirit-given. In humans, natural selection has become actual selection. We are the species that is able to select our future. This creative principle (we call it the Logos or Wisdom of God) has an interior dimension to it—it has consciousness, and guess what. You are it. It is you. The sacred evolutionary impulse has awakened, come to consciousness, in a particular occasion and process, packaged in a particular body, and it's wearing your name. It's the most real thing about you and about us.

Why do we always refer back two thousand years and claim that Jesus was the only human who incarnated this impulse? Jesus would laugh at this claim. It was flowing through him, and he tried to help his disciples realize that it was flowing through them as well. It *was* them. This energy can be frightening. The first disciples had trouble believing it because they didn't want the responsibility of knowing that the power to co-create the future was theirs to manifest. "No one who puts a hand to the plough and looks back," Jesus said, "is fit for the kingdom of God" (Luke 9:62). Jesus doesn't want us looking back, because the sacred evolutionary impulse is future-oriented. This is why forgiveness is such a central spiritual practice. We forgive not to feel good about ourselves or even for the sake of whoever has hurt us; we forgive so that we can be released from the past in order to co-create the future.[3]

"I am about to do a new thing," says the prophet Isaiah on God's behalf, "now it springs forth, do you not perceive it?" (Isaiah 43:19).

Theologically and ecclesiologically, we still act as though all the real action took place in Jerusalem two thousand years ago, and we're just waiting for what God did back then in Jesus to play itself out. Well, it's taking place right here, right now.

"No problem," said Einstein, "can be solved from the same level of consciousness that created it." Yes, the world is in trouble. Yes, there is injustice. Yes, there is war and violence. Yes, the planet is in serious trouble. But we need to bring to these problems a transformed self, a soul-full self, a Christ-animated self. We need, each of us in our own unique way, to put on the Heart and Mind of Christ. We need to know what Christ consciousness feels like from the inside before we continue our crusade to change the world.

Think of the voice of the gardener in the parable as the voice of the Christ—speaking to us at those moments when we've given up hope—in ourselves and in our congregations. It's Christ's voice,

---

[3] See "Why Forgive?" (page 65) for more on forgiveness.

all right, speaking to us from the *future*, which needs us in order to emerge; speaking to us from the *past*, our roots reaching deep into the soil of tradition; speaking to us *now*, as the sap of the evolutionary impulse to grow, to bear fruit, to be God's people in the world and for the world. By the grace of God, a Cosmic Gardener who is our gardener and advocate, our fruit bearing has just begun.

God as Future

Exodus 3:1-17

Theologian John Haught suggests that the best name for God, a name that is grounded in the scriptural narrative, is the Future.[1] The idea of God inhabiting the future is harder to grasp than the idea of God inhabiting the past or the present. We have history books, our own personal history, and memory to assure us of the reality of the past. It's stuff that happened already. The present is not a problem for us either; the present seems undeniable, if only because of our apparent incapacity to dwell fully in it, as Eckhart Tolle and other gurus of the "now" remind us. The present is this moment and we are able to experience it by breathing deeply, stopping our chattering mind, and inhabiting our experiences.

But this moment is also always about to intersect with a future that is always in the process of arriving. There, it just arrived again. But we have difficulty granting full, existential status to the future, because the future, by definition, doesn't exist yet. Unlike the past and present, it has no content. Yet, it just arrived again. And the moment it arrives, it is no longer the future. The future is always just beyond our grasp, yet it is always in the process of arriving.

In the Book of Revelation, God is referred to as Alpha, the beginning, and Omega, the end (Revelation 1:8). We have tended to

---

[1] John Haught, *God After Darwin: A Theology of Evolution* (Philadelphia: Westview Press, 2008), 105–108 and 214–217.

privilege God as Alpha—Creator. But we haven't done much thinking about how God is present as Omega—the end. Fundamentalist religion does think about God as Omega, but to these folks, it means that God has fixed a predetermined end time when "He" will bring the world to an abrupt and violent end. This way of thinking renders the past and the present as little more than filler. It's just what happens while we're waiting around for the real action—apocalyptic action—to take place. It diminishes the role of history and our personal role in shaping the future.

Catholic priest and palaeontologist Pierre Teilhard de Chardin was a progressive thinker who took both evolution and the future seriously. He asked the question, "Who will at last give evolution its God?"[2] He was looking for a way to imagine God that honoured science and, particularly, evolutionary science. To truly honour evolution, especially *conscious* evolution in the human species, is to grant us the capacity to make choices that really make a difference. We are not waiting around for some sky-God to unilaterally intervene with a predetermined future. We are the ones who are able to consciously co-create the future. At the same time, we as Christians assert that the Reality we call God is free to influence our choices in a non-coercive way. Teilhard de Chardin imagined a cosmic Christ as the *Omega* Point, and not just the Alpha. The Omega Point is the alluring presence of the future, to which all of creation is converging and, in the process of this convergence, is evolving in intelligence, love, and creativity.

Teilhard de Chardin imagined God as a divine milieu encompassing and insinuating Her/Him/Itself into the past, the present, *and* the future. God is present in the past as the One and the Oneness from whom a universe emerged. This is the God witnessed to in the great scriptures of the world's religions, and in the ancient tribal myths and legends of indigenous people. The more theologically conserva-

---

[2] Pierre Teilhard de Chardin, *Christianity and Evolution: Reflections on Science and Religion*, trans. Rene Hague (New York: Harcourt, Brace and Co., 1969), 240.

tive that one is, the greater the tendency to locate what we can know about God exclusively in these historic narratives, or indeed within the tradition that organizes itself around these narratives. When the past is privileged as a way of knowing God, we look back at the scripture, at the tradition, and at the historic founder—in our case, Jesus of Nazareth—for revelation and truth.[3]

We can also know God in the present. The universe is eternally in the process of arising anew in every moment. Books like Tolle's *Power of Now* are popular with postmodern types who declare themselves to be "spiritual but not religious." What this means is that they are not particularly interested in looking back in time to experience the sacred. Rather, they seek liberation from the past and the future in the stillness of the "timeless" now. By inhabiting this moment, we free ourselves from the tyranny of our minds and our worries about the future. Meditation helps us to enter this state of consciousness that is all about abiding in the present. We discover a sense of the sacred in attending deeply to, and honouring, whatever is arising now and now and now.

But can God also arise as the One who is present in the unrehearsed and indeterminate future? The biblical witness seems to contend that this is, in fact, where God hangs out—not so much "up above," but out in front. I'll come back to this, but for now, we need to remind ourselves of what is at stake here. We are claiming that God

---

[3] Science tends to privilege the past as well in its assumption that everything that exists was caused by something that happened in the past. Historical causality is an unexamined assumption of science, looking to the past to explain what can emerge in the future. Radical materialists, like Richard Dawkins and Daniel Dennett, assume that the DNA molecule that was formed billions of years ago is responsible in an absolute fashion for determining the future. This is called genetic determinism. But you need to go back even further, they claim; the foundations of life as we know it today must be traced back to the absolute simplest atoms that emerged from the big bang 13.7 billion years ago. No greater power is allowed—not *within* those helium and hydrogen atoms, and not *without*. Deep time, the random collision of atoms, and natural laws account for complex consciousness and civilization as we know it today. Many scientists who have trouble accounting for the emergence of mind from matter claim that free will—our attempt to shape a future different from the past through conscious choice—is an illusion, that the future is determined by the material past in an absolute fashion.

is somehow present in a future that doesn't exist yet. Furthermore, we are requiring that God be present in this future in such a way that honours the free will and the evolutionary creativity of human beings—given that we are the evolutionary impulse of the universe in personalized form. In other words, as a matter of principle, and by way of dignifying free will, no future can be imposed upon us. God must be present in the future in such a way that influences, but does not interfere in, the evolution of the universe.

This idea that God is present in the future is grounded in Scripture. There are countless stories of God alluring God's people forward in and through a promise of a better future, a future that needs them in order for it to be realized. For example, the legend of the liberation of the Hebrew people from Egyptian slavery imagines God as being out in front, taking the lead. God is the presence of the future that visits Moses in a burning bush. That future, in God's mind, consists of a world that is free of slavery and the kind of suffering that the Hebrews are enduring. This idea "comes" to Moses as a possibility that hadn't entered his head. Then, when Moses asks for the name of the God who is about to confront Pharaoh, the divine name can be translated as "I am Who I am" or "I will be Who I will be"—the One who is both Present and Future.

This Presence enters the consciousness of Moses with the provocation to set the Hebrews free. Where did the idea come from? The narrative implies that it came from the God who dwells in the realm of future possibilities that have not yet been considered by humans. How on Earth, Moses wants to know, can he possibly take on the pharaoh of Egypt? God simply asks Moses to trust that it's possible. And after a series of confrontations with the pharaoh, along with deadly plagues, the Hebrews make their great escape. The legend of this escape affirms that God went *ahead* of them, in a pillar of fire by night, and a cloud by day, so that they could travel day and night toward the Future's promise of freedom.

In the Bible, God is always imagined to be out in front, leading from and toward a future that the people haven't imagined is possible. Typically, life conditions are such that the present is bleak, and nobody in their right mind would want to inhabit it more deeply. Embracing the spirituality of the now would have been absurd. When the boot of history is firmly planted on your neck, to abide in the present is to welcome a broken neck. What was required was hope in the future, and so God is consistently portrayed as meeting those who cared to listen as the Presence of a preferred future in the here and now.

It is not a deep acceptance of present conditions that is the source of the hope; it's the glimpse into a new future that enables the Jewish people to keep going. By some mystery, Moses gets it into his head that the current circumstances of oppression are not God's intention for the Hebrew people—and he so deeply owns that possibility that he takes responsibility for its realization. If there is any miracle in the Bible, this is it—this dynamic of the future coming to meet certain individuals with new possibilities, and those people being so transformed by the possibilities that they step up and consent to the future's realization occurring in and through them. God is present in the future as the elicitor or provocateur of fresh possibilities. God comes to God's people from the future, opening up space to imagine and enact new possibilities through conscious consent. Moses is free to refuse to act on this glimpse of an alternative future, as we all are.

But how can God be present in and as the Future in a way that doesn't overpower our free will and unilaterally determine that future? Can science help us here? If evolution is to have its own God, we must be able to find analogies in the realm of science. We might find some help in what science is simply recognizing as "information."[4] For our purposes, information refers to the capacity of the universe to bring higher order from lower order. There is a power that is distinct from

---

[4] Haught, *God After Darwin*, 81–84.

both matter and energy—what physicist David Bohm calls a hidden wholeness[5]—that pervades reality with a tendency to bring coherence, integrity, and complexity from relative disorder. Science acknowledges this mystery with words like *novelty, self-organization*, and *autopoiesis*. Novelty means that when two parts come together, the whole that forms is not only greater than the sum of the parts, but it is also unpredictably novel and more complex. Self-organization means that a system under pressure may escape to a *higher* order. Autopoiesis refers to the capacity of an organism to self-renew or change. But let's not confuse description with explanation. Science has words for it, but information remains a mystery.

Life just seems to know how to do life. From matter, life arises; from life, mind arises; from mind, self-conscious awareness arises; and from self-conscious awareness (by which a universe comes to know itself), responsibility to choose and work toward a desired future arises. Hardcore materialists claim that the more complex levels emerged out of the simplest forms. Dirt somehow pulled itself up by its own bootstraps and learned how to do nuclear physics. This so-called bootstrapping theory implies an ordering or patterning field of information that exerts an upward or forward pull to influence reality toward greater unity and diversity and consciousness. This process can be imagined as more than the erotic push of the evolutionary impulse. It is also an alluring pull from the future. Information exists as a realm of higher or greater possibility that influences, but doesn't interfere with, evolutionary processes.

This provides an interesting analogy for how God may be present as a noninterfering yet active presence that comes to us from the realm of the future. I'm not equating information with God, but merely suggesting that it's a functional analogy. John Haught compares this informational or ordering capacity of the universe to what the Taoists call

---

[5] "Quantum Bohmian Mechanics: David Bohm," On Truth & Reality, accessed November 20, 2011, http://spaceandmotion.com/physics-quantum-bohmian-mechanics.htm.

wu-wei, the wayless way. The Tao is energetically passive but informationally active. It is active inaction or noninterfering effectiveness.[6]

Gaze at it; there is nothing to see.
It is called the formless.
Heed it; there is nothing to hear.
It is called the soundless.
Grasp it; there is nothing to hold on to.
It is called the immaterial.
Invisible, it cannot be called by name.
It returns again to nothingness.[7]

All religious and spiritual lineages throughout the ages have affirmed that the higher order cannot emerge from the lower. Again, what scientists call the spontaneous emergence of higher order from the lower is merely descriptive. If science introduces the idea of information to explain this mystery, then theology is certainly within its rights to use this analogy to describe how God influences the world without being an interfering presence. Indeed, Paul talks about how God's power is made manifest in weakness (2 Corinthians 12:9) and how God empties Godself of power *as force* in order to be present as the alluring power of Love (Philippians 2:1–8). John Caputo is developing a theology based on the weakness of God.[8] God is the Something that is present as the influential no-thing—for those who have eyes to see, ears to hear, and hearts that are open. God empties Godself of power as force precisely by withdrawing into the future that is always coming toward us with new possibilities for higher order, new ways of being—more aligned with Love Itself.

We have trouble grasping this concept because we have been trained to think of only the past and present as "really real." We have been steeped in historical causality. Everything that we see around us must have been caused by some event in the past. Indeed, much

---

[6] Haught, *God After Darwin*, 77–80.

[7] Ibid., 80.

[8] John D. Caputo, *The Weakness of God: A Theology of the Event* (Bloomington: Indiana University Press, 2006).

of our life is correlated to our past. But is it absolutely caused by the past? Maybe not. Look at our language. We wonder what the future "holds." In this metaphor of holding, the future is a container of untold possibilities. It's not predetermined, but rather comes to us through intuition, in glimpses, and through unexpected opportunities and circumstances that "present" themselves to us. If we're open to them, we discover within them an invisible, intangible, powerful creativity to reshape our own lives and also the future of Earth itself. The future is always beyond us—as is God—and yet it is forever coming toward us with an offer of new life.

Isn't it legitimate to speak not just of historical causality but also of future causality—the future causing us to act in a new way *now* in response to a promise of something better? We're not simply determined by the past, but also by an alluring promise of the future. God is in that promise of the future as much as God is in the past and the present. Theologian Paul Tillich defined faith as willingness to be apprehended by the future.[9]

This is the gospel in a nutshell. It is the story of Easter. The future seems to close down on the disciples when the death-dealing forces of history—the force of the empire and the need for absolute control—crucify Jesus. But when they arrive at the tomb, an angelic messenger—symbolizing the future—tells them that they'll have to look somewhere other than a tomb if they want to find Jesus. He has *gone ahead* of them to Galilee (Matthew 28:10). Like a living pillar of fire by night and a cloud by day, the divine is always going on ahead of us, drawing us toward a promise that will not be snuffed out by the power of death and violence. When fate has played its trump card, Galilee is our rendezvous with hope.

Followers of the Christ are always on the way to Galilee, drawn by the promise of a coming order that may shatter, confirm, or reorganize the existing order of our lives. This is what gives us hope when our

---

[9] Paul Tillich, *The Eternal Now* (New York: Charles Scribner's Songs, 1963).

personal and planetary lives are falling apart. This is how we evolve. It matters more now than at any other time on our planet that we take hold of this future that is holding us—that we consent to be apprehended by this hope, and we each find our unique way of saying yes to God's promise that God has gone ahead of us, and yet is always coming to meet us.

Finding Your Inner Shepherd

Psalm 23, John 10:1–10

In Psalm 23, God is the Shepherd. In the reading from John's gospel, Jesus plays that role. When the spiritual journey is imagined as being primarily about following (a moral path, a way of truth, a teaching or a teacher), then the metaphor of the Good Shepherd leading the sheep makes a lot of sense. Not so long ago, I thought that this metaphor had outlived its usefulness and belonged to another day and age. Then my wife and I travelled to New Zealand and discovered that shepherding is a university course.

The novice sojourner is like a sheep, unfamiliar with the territory and needing somebody to look out for her. Many people walk through the door of Canadian Memorial, for example, honouring an impulse to find a spiritual path. But they don't know the congregation or our beliefs. They may not even be clear about what they are looking for. Something is drawing them, but they might not be able to articulate it. All they have to go on is their intuition: Can I trust this congregation? Do I like the sound of his voice? Are these people friendly? These folks are like sheep in search of a community to act as shepherd and guide them through some unfamiliar terrain.

I feel great compassion for the contemporary seeker of spirituality. Many young people have no spiritual tradition. They are not predisposed to trust a particular teaching or a particular tradition—especially Christianity, which is at an all-time low in terms of public trust.

To use the ancient metaphor from John's gospel, they walk through the "gate" (front door) of the church, and they are vulnerable, like sheep in the midst of wolves. We know we're not wolves, but they don't. So, for those who might feel a little vulnerable as seekers of spirituality, this is my Sheep's Guide to Sniffing Out Bad Religion:

- If you don't feel love in the place, don't hang around.
- Love is not enough. Warm and fuzzy only takes you so far. Cults are pretty good at warm and fuzzy.
- If you get the sense that the folks there have set answers to your deep questions, leave. Your questions will become your inner shepherd, guiding you into truth. You want a community that is fascinated by your questions and will support you as you let the questions be your shepherd.
- Listen carefully for whether the folks are inwardly focused on themselves or outwardly focused on serving the larger community. You want to find a flock of people who are growing both inwardly, deepening their spiritual identity, and also opening their hearts to the suffering in the world.
- If you hear somebody, anybody, quote Scripture as a way of excluding certain groups of people—such as women, or gays and lesbians—from full and equal leadership in church, run, don't walk. Scripture was never meant to be used like this.
- If the leader makes you feel like a bad person and then provides a magic formula or some set of beliefs that is going to save you or make you part of the in-group (God's elect), leave.
- If religion and science are pitted against each other and you are asked to believe stuff you know isn't true, don't waste your time. When the Bible says that the world was created in seven days, it's not intended as a scientific fact, and if somebody tries to sell you this, trust your rational

faculties, thank the nice man at the door, leave, and don't go back.

In the reading, John's gospel presents Jesus as saying that he is the Good Shepherd. That's fine, and I'm convinced that Jesus is indeed a trustworthy leader. I've given my life to following his teachings. But it's unlikely that Jesus ever said the words that are in the reading. Which is a good thing, because there are parts of the reading that are actually nasty.

The author of John's gospel put these words on the lips of Jesus, and this fellow had a pretty large bone to pick with his Jewish brothers and sisters who didn't believe that Jesus was the Messiah. He and his community had likely been banned from synagogue for this belief, and he was not pleased. Sometimes, John's writing soars with spiritual insight. Usually, this is when he is not trashing his fellow Jews. We need to bring awareness of the author's bias and context whenever we read John's gospel.

Jesus is presented, for example, as the only valid gatekeeper. Other shepherds—spiritual leaders and, in particular, Jews—are called thieves and bandits. They come only to "kill and destroy" (John 10:10). Countless generations of Christians have used this passage to invalidate other religious paths. The early church fathers used passages like these to invalidate and persecute Christian leaders whom they regarded as heretics. And because, in other places in his gospel, the writer of John's gospel explicitly identifies the thieves and bandits as Jews, who killed and destroyed Jesus, the church has a shameful history of persecuting Jews.

Which leads me to add this to my Sheep's Guide to Sniffing Out Bad Religion:

- If a church refuses to bring a critical perspective to its own Scripture, it's a sign to find another Shepherd.

So, let me be clear. There is a time and a place for shepherding in the church. The religion founded in Jesus's name needs to be willing and able to assume a shepherding role—especially for people who are new to the spiritual path. People need guidance through treacherous passages of life, protection from charlatans and snake-oil salesmen, and they need a safe place to rest when they are weary.

But at some point, it becomes a natural evolutionary step to find our own inner shepherd. If a religion, any religion, keeps you in the role of the sheep for a lifetime, it is not of God, and it is certainly not in the spirit of the Christ. Which brings me to my next point of discernment of whether you've found the right spiritual community:

- The right spiritual community encourages you to grow up. It provides a path to spiritual maturity. In evolutionary spirituality, this is the "path of righteousness." It leads you forward into the future, and not simply home, dragging your tail behind you.

This is spiritual evolution. This is always in the direction of assuming increasing levels of responsibility for the quality and direction of your own life, for the cultures that we inhabit, and for the social systems in which we are embedded. To be in Christ to is to discover your inner shepherd and your inner authority. You will carefully listen to the experience and wisdom of others, of course. But you will measure it against an inner compass. After listening, you will ask yourself: Is this true for me? You will learn to trust your spiritual intuition and the subtle energies in your body to help you clarify your next best step.

Parker Palmer, a Quaker and teacher of the spiritual path, painfully made this discovery for himself. After a life of looking outside of himself for God's will and trying to be the person he imagined everybody else, including God, thought he should be, he went into a deep, clinical depression. He tells his story in his aptly named book, *Let Your Life Speak*. He emerged from depression by accepting that his own life, inside and out, was his surest guide to abundant life. He listened to his inner stirrings, to what gave him joy, to the doors that closed in his face, and to the ones that opened. He dropped his persona of living for status and to please others. He discovered the quirky uniqueness that made him Parker Palmer and realized that this was the image of God within him. And then, he let that be his inner guide for how to do life. He became his own Good Shepherd. His depression lifted.[1]

As you grow in spiritual maturity, you will read Psalm 23 and understand that the Lord who is your Shepherd shows up not only as an external source of authority but as the deepest aspect of your inner being. You will gain the maturity to know when it is time to take yourself to green pastures, you will know where these pastures are located, and you will lay yourself down in them. You will know how to access the "still waters" of Pure Conscious Awareness. You will feel from the inside out when it is time to restore your soul. You will have an inner conviction of what is the path of righteousness—of the right relationship with All That Is. As you grow in spiritual maturity, fear will be less and less of a determinative emotion in your life. You will "fear no evil" because you will know that Love alone is eternal. Your security will be grounded, not in material wealth and insurance policies, but in the deep knowledge that you "dwell in the house of the Lord" (the abiding presence of God), always have and always will.

You will know that God is All, and when it is your time to pass through even the darkest valleys, you will know that this, too, is happening in God—as it was for Parker Palmer. The darkness had to deepen, in fact, before he would listen. You will know that life is a cup that is continually filling up and spilling over because this is just what the universe does in every moment. The universe is filling up and spilling over in the radiant manifestation that wears your blessed name. One day, you will awaken to the startling truth that you are an occasion of That which you have been seeking. And God willing, one day you may feel it as your vocation to be Good Shepherd to a lost and lonely soul who is just finding her way back to the Heart and Mind

---

[1] Parker J. Palmer, *Let Your Life Speak: Listening for the Voice of Vocation* (San Francisco: Jossey-Bass, 2000), 56–72.

of God. And then you will truly know what it is to have goodness and mercy follow you all the days of your life.

The Return of the Prodigal Species

Luke 15:11–32

The youngest son impetuously demands his inheritance—what is already his but what he can't wait to receive—and leaves home. It's interesting to treat this story as the parable of the prodigal *species*. In the past three hundred years, we have grabbed the 13.7 billion years of sacred inheritance, embodied as Earth, and, like the prodigal son, we are in the process of squandering it. From one perspective, this represents a kind of hubris.

But from another perspective, this leaving home was a necessary, if high stakes, phase of our evolutionary development as a species. It is the hero's journey: leaving home and facing all manner of ordeals, so that when it comes time to return home, it is with a new identity. The heroic journey is transformative. The hero paves the evolutionary path forward for those who, like the elder brother, stayed home out of a sense of duty or obligation. From a psychological point of view, adolescents need to rebel in order to sufficiently individuate and become their own persons. From a socio-cultural view, we can see the evolutionary necessity of humanity taking the hero's journey and leaving a naive premodern identification with nature and her processes in order to realize our unique potentials. This describes the human journey into the modernist worldview.

The problem is that this modernist project of distinguishing ourselves from nature descended into disconnection from the planet and into a full psychotic state of disassociation?[1] In this state, we are in the process of foolishly destroying our very source of life.

Evolutionary theology posits that the problem with humanity is not that we are innately sinful but rather that we are in a stage of adolescence as a species, acting very badly. We've been around for about 200,000 years as humans. This might seem like a long time in a human timescale, but in cosmic time, this is a snap of the fingers. Our brains and biochemistry are still locked for most of our waking hours in the crocodile brain, which is in a constant state of red alert—focused solely on our own survival. We are not bad. But we're treating Earth, her creatures, and her biosystems as though they belong to us. It's actually the other way around—we belong to Earth. But in a dissociated modernist state of consciousness, we forgot that we are one part of a larger ecosystem and that our fate is inextricably linked to it. We turned nature into a natural resource. We lost a sense of awe and wonder at the living system of Earth. Philosopher and theologian Abraham Heschel wrote: "Forfeit your sense of awe . . . and the universe becomes a market place for you."[2]

From the perspective of our wisdom tradition, our problem is not that we are sinners but that we are foolish. We always need to remember, as philosopher Ken Wilber puts it, that in an evolutionary paradigm, humanity has not so much fallen from an original Paradise as we have been moving "up from Eden"[3]—we are the universe moving in an upward trajectory of increasing empathy. Our ecological intelligence, however, is lagging.

We are the prodigal species. What began as a hero's journey to realize new potentials by individuating ourselves from naive identification

---

[1] Ken Wilber, *Sex, Ecology, Spirituality: The Spirit of Evolution* (Boston: Shambala Publications, Inc., 2000).

[2] Abraham Joshua Heschel, *God in Search of Man: A Philosophy of Judaism* (Toronto: Douglas & McIntyre Ltd., 1983), 78.

[3] Ken Wilber, *Up From Eden: A Transpersonal View of Human Evolution* (Garden City, NY: Anchor Press/Doubleday, 1981).

with nature descended into a dissociative state. We are in the midst of squandering 13.7 billion years in less than three hundred years. We are, like the prodigal son, living in a pigpen of our own making. As a Jew, he was rendered unclean by his contact with Gentiles and, particularly, with pigs. As human beings at the top of the food chain, our own bodies are filled with toxins. Having spoiled Earth, we are now impure. So great is our state of alienation that we thought we could just throw stuff away, but as Julia Butterfly Hill so poignantly asks: "Where is *away*?"[4]

In a unified, universe, there is no away. Whatever we imagine we are throwing away—into our rivers, oceans, earth, air—will end up in our own bodies and our children's bodies.

The good news is that we are each one of Wisdom's children, as Jesus called himself. We can learn. We evolve. Within us is all the resilience of this magnificent cosmos, which is enveloped and infused by a creative intelligence that is able to adapt to changing life conditions. This process of adapting to challenges is what drives evolution at all levels: biological, social, cultural, and spiritual.

It is his own survival instinct that causes the prodigal son to come to his senses. He's hungry. Nobody gives him anything to eat. His father's slaves are living a better life. He is in a full-blown crisis, which, in an evolutionary worldview, is not the end of the world. Potentially, it's the beginning of a new future. I find in this evolutionary theology an implicit hopefulness. There are no guarantees, of course, and the trajectory is not smooth or linear. According to one theory, evolutionary leaps occur through a process know as punctuated equilibrium, whereby evolution plateaus for long periods of time and then leaps forward—not incrementally but dramatically. In the presence of crises, these leaps may occur.[5]

---

[4] "Where is Away?" YouTube video; 1:56, posted by feelgoodworld, August 31, 2010, http://www.youtube.com/watch?v=UJARRREipmI.

[5] Niles Eldredge and S.J. Gould, "Punctuated Equilibria: An Alternative to Phyletic Gradualism," in N. Eldredge, *Time Frames* (Princeton: Princeton University Press, 1985), 193–223.

This ecological crisis we are facing has the potential to elicit new intelligences, new behaviours, and new technologies that could issue in the emergence of a new kind of human presence—the ecological human, if you like. It may not, of course. By 2020, the so-called "adversity trends" may "coalesce into an unyielding, world-scale systems crisis. Every major system in our lives—ecological, economic, political, cultural, psychological, and spiritual—will be in crisis as it is challenged to adapt to a dramatically changing world."[6]

At this point in the evolution of the universe, it is truly our choice. We are a particular expression of the universe, a mode of planetary presence that represents what Brian Swimme calls a macrophase power.[7] Earth has never had to contend with a force like the human species, which has such power to destroy.

On the other hand, we may come to our senses and learn the ways of Wisdom. In our tradition, Sophia is the feminine personification of sacred Wisdom. An ancient Gnostic cosmology understands Wisdom to have incarnated as Earth. Dr. Sallie McFague invites us to imagine Earth as God's body.[8]

To listen to Wisdom, in the twenty-first century, is to connect more deeply with the intelligence of Earth. Our planet has almost five billions years of wisdom stored up. She possesses an immense intelligence that can help us survive this crisis. "Ask the animals, and they will teach you; the birds of the air, and they will tell you; ask the plants of the earth, and they will teach you; and the fish of the sea will declare to you" (Job 12:7–8).

In Janine Benyus's brilliant book *Biomimicry,* she documents how we're just beginning to listen. Biomimicry is the emerging practice of

---

[6] Duane Elgin, *The Living Universe: Where Are We? Who Are We? Where Are We Going?* (San Francisco: Berrett-Koehler Publishers, Inc., 2009), 139.

[7] Brian Swimme, *The Hidden Heart of the Cosmos: Humanity and the New Story* (New York: Orbis Books, 1996).

[8] Sallie McFague, *The Body of God: An Ecological Theology* (Minneapolis: Fortress Press, 1993).

learning to mimic Earth's processes in the development of new technology, social systems, and building. Her book is filled with examples of the intelligence of Earth's processes. Scientists, farmers, and architects are just now beginning to realize that by imitating natural processes, we can thrive in all areas of life.[9]

The honeybee has learned to support its biosystem in the process of building its society. Bees take nothing from Earth that they don't return. In Dr. Marilyn Hamilton's groundbreaking book, *Integral City: Evolutionary Intelligences for the Human Hive,* she suggests that we would do well to mimic the honeybee in our design of the city as an ecosystem.[10]

The honeybee has developed an intelligent learning-feedback loop. A bee is not focused on itself but on the survival of the hive. And in the process of helping the hive, the bee sustains not just the individual or even its own hive, but it adds value to (as opposed to extracting life from) the flowers, fields, and orchards that it pollinates. Marilyn is helping city planners design cities like the honeybee designs its hive. When we understand the nature of this one Earth community, we realize that nature has figured out how to sync up the multiple intelligences of the diverse species and ecosystems so that the whole organism can thrive. Coming to our senses means first noticing, and then mimicking, the planet's deep adaptive intelligence.

A member of our congregation has a cherry tree that hadn't produced fruit for years. The tree surgeon recommended cutting it down. But Angela had heard about a species of local bees that might be able to save it. So she bought a hive and set it up in her front yard near the tree. This past year, they picked more than fifty pounds of cherries from that tree. She applied a natural wisdom to the crisis of her cherry tree, and it worked.

---

[9] Janine Benyus, *Biomimicry: Innovation Inspired by Nature* (New York: Harper Perennial, 1997).

[10] Marilyn Hamilton, *Integral City: Evolutionary Intelligences for the Human Hive* (Gabriola Island: New Society Publishers, 2008).

William McDonough is an architectural engineer who has gone radically green in his practice. He works with major corporations, like the Ford Motor Company, with a simple, natural principle. He noticed that in nature, there is no waste. In nature, waste equals food. He worked with a textile company in Switzerland to help them resource only natural, organic dyes, and then to develop a processing system so that the water that comes out at the end of the manufacturing process is more pure than the water that went into the process at the beginning.

He calls this cradle-to-cradle engineering.[11] Everything a company produces is returned to the company at the end of the product's lifecycle. This gives the company incentive to produce products that are radically reusable and recyclable. Everything we produce comes back to us—and that cycle is true for good or ill. If we are unconscious of this natural intelligence, and what we produce is toxic and draws down the natural capital of the planet, then it will eventually kill us. But if we collaborate with the natural, sacred intelligence of the planet, then what comes back to us after production will enhance us and all of life.

The prodigal son returns home, having come to his senses, with a changed identity. He has undergone a change of heart. No longer the entitled son, he prepares his homecoming speech from the perspective of a servant ("I am no longer worthy to be called your son"). In a similar fashion, the human species needs to undergo a fundamental shift in identity—from the privileged species who can take whatever we want, when we want it, and dispose of our waste wherever we want, to life-enhancing servants of our awesome planet.

But before he is able to get the full speech out of his mouth, his father has him in a bear hug and is smothering him with kisses. His son that was lost is now found. Let us pray that Earth and all of our kin species are as generous with us as we make our way back home to the heart of the cosmos.

---

[11] William McDonough and Michael Braungart, *Cradle to Cradle: Remaking the Way We Make Things* (New York: North Point Press, 2002).

Disturbing the Peace

Matthew 5:1–10 and 10:34–39, Luke 12:49–51

To inaugurate the International Day of Peace, which occurs annually on September 21, the Peace Bell is rung at the United Nations Headquarters in New York City. The bell is cast from coins donated by children from all continents, and it was given to the UN as a gift from Japan as "a reminder of the human cost of war." The inscription on its side reads: "Long live absolute peace."[1]

I don't know what "absolute peace" means. I find peace almost impossible to define. You can define it *as* a *state* of consciousness (inner peace or bliss), or *through* a *stage* of consciousness (tribal, warrior, modern, postmodern worldviews). You can define it *from* the perspective of self, culture, nature, and social systems. Ideally, in an integral frame, you'd include all of these. But that definition would end up being an entire book, which is probably why the default definition of peace is the absence of war.

What I've come to realize is that I don't actually believe in peace. What I mean is that I don't believe in peace as it is commonly imagined. Obviously, I believe that the absence of armed conflict is desirable. But even if we were able to bring all armed conflict to an end, why are we ending conflict? I'm not convinced that world peace is the end game.

---

[1] "Secretary-General's remarks at the ringing of the Peace Bell for the International Day of Peace," September 20, 2002, the United Nations Secretary-General's Statements, accessed November 13, 2011, http://www.un.org/apps/sg/sgstats.asp?nid=71.

In evolutionary spirituality, the end game is the advance of whatever we imagine to be our highest ideal—for example, the advance of Love. But this advance is never actually "peaceful." More often than not, it involves disturbing the peace. Jesus was executed for the crime of disturbing the peace. The peacemakers may be *blessed*, as Jesus claims in Matthew's gospel (Matthew 5:9), but it's God who blesses them, and rarely the system that they are disturbing. The Roman Peace—*pax Romana*—was a peace established and maintained through violence, not a peace through justice. So the particular social equilibrium called the Roman Empire was in need of disturbing. Rosa Parks, Martin Luther King Jr., Gandhi, Betty Friedan, and Aung San Suu Kyi, all of these heroes disturbed the peace, and what they ultimately wanted was not the mere absence of conflict, but the evolution of entrenched systems of racism, authoritarianism, and patriarchy.

Peacemaking is rarely peaceful. Perhaps a cosmological analogy will help. We're not sure if Earth is the only planet in the universe to come to life, but we're pretty certain that it's the only planet in our solar system to achieve life. Jupiter is so large that its mass doesn't allow for its gases to cool and form matter. It's basically a ball of gas that will never evolve. Mars, on the other hand, got as far as boulders, but it lacks sufficient inner turbulence for it to evolve into life. Earth is the perfect size—neither too big nor too small, neither too hot nor too cool. It's the Goldilocks story of our solar system. The crust and surface of Earth is solid enough to support life. But deep within, a molten iron core that is constantly churning fires Earth. Every once in a while this liquid fire breaks though the crust in the form an active volcano, reminding us that the secret of life is this slow burn—or what cosmologists call balanced turbulence, which no other planet enjoys. It's this balanced turbulence that allows life to evolve.

When most people think about peace, they imagine the absence of turbulence. They imagine their religion as the one unchanging rock in the midst of flux. But when they imagine an unchanging rock, they are imagining Mars. Many people come to church because they want to find "peace." That's understandable. Life can feel overwhelming. But, in truth, the church doesn't exist to provide peace—at least, that's not the end game. The church is here to provide just enough of that kind of peace so that those who do feel overwhelmed can rest long enough to get back to the true business of evolving.

If you define peace as absolute stillness and calm, there won't be enough fire to fuel our project of evolutionary transcendence. Through meditation it's possible to achieve a state of absolute stillness. You literally experience your self before you were born. You are in a state of Pure Being, before a universe began. It is a deeply restful place because you are free from suffering, free from worry, and free from all desire. This is because you aren't actually in the world. You are pre-world, pre-time, pre–big bang, pre-form.

This is a good, useful, and time-honoured practice—I rest in this eternal stillness myself every day—but the moment you come out of the meditation and enter into this universe, you will be apprehended by an impulse to evolve. Everything in the universe is caught up in an impulse to transcend itself. This is simply a condition of the universe, and since you are the universe having a human experience, you are the part of the universe that is able to consciously engage in the project of self-transcendence. That's what your freedom is for. That's what God wants of you. Become a better, fuller, freer, more loving expression of yourself (in community with others) and thereby serve the evolution of the universe.

The way that life transcends itself in every realm is to dynamically move between two poles: these two poles are unity at the one end, and diversity or differentiation at the other; other words you could use for this polarity are *communion* and *autonomy*, or *receptivity* and *agency*. My problem with peace in popular understanding is that it tends to get stuck in the unity, communion, and receptive end of the continuum. Peace is unity. Peace is being one with everything. Peace is harmony.

But I wonder what Jesus meant when he was recorded as saying:

> I came to bring fire to the earth, and how I wish that it were already kindled. I have a baptism with which to be baptized, and what stress I am under until it is completed! Do you think that I have come to give peace to the earth? No, I tell you, but rather division! (Luke 12:49–51)

Or again, when he says, "I have not come to bring peace, but a sword" (Matthew 10:34). He then goes on to describe how he wants to divide a family.

Fire? Swords? Division? The reason we have such difficulty with these sayings is that we've exclusively associated peace with the unifying, harmonious end of the continuum. But a lot of our commitment to oneness comes at the expense of our commitment to differentiation, self-expression, and, ultimately, evolution. Jesus is not advocating violence. He's introducing more turbulence into a system that is frozen into a form that is not serving life.

So if peace is going to be real, it needs to be imagined as a state of dynamic equilibrium (or balanced turbulence). Scientists will tell you that a system in perfect equilibrium is the definition of death. Instead, you want to create a life that is an optimal culture or container for the flow between these two poles. On our planet right now, the life force is trying to rebalance itself through turbulence, and human beings will only change when the pain of remaining the same becomes greater than the pain of evolving. The so-called Arab Spring arose from the fact that a series of Middle Eastern dictators defined peace as absolute stability. Libya, Egypt, Syria, and Yemen have been statehood's equivalent of Mars: stable, but unable to evolve. The people are ready to grow up, but men like Muammar Gaddafi (Libya), Hosni Mubarak (Egypt), Bashar al-Assad (Syria), and Ali Abdullah Saleh (Yemen) were and are actively and wilfully refusing the natural impulse to mature. Each of them interpreted stability as keeping power in the family throughout the generations, and liberally used violence and the threat of violence to keep the peace. But the life force will always rise up to break this artificially imposed evolutionary truce. It rises up in the people's urge to differentiate from the regime. The people want to be heard and seen as individuals. It's the modernist impulse and it won't be denied. These ordinary citizens rising up to challenge the system represent the universal life urge to transcend—in this case, it's a political transcendence of a system that is not complex enough for twenty-first-century modernist culture.

The peacemakers of the twenty-first century are wizards at knowing when and how to intervene in an entrenched system that is unable to evolve. Peacemakers are not in the service of absolute peace but of the evolution of self, culture, and social systems. Sometimes we need to introduce the sword of differentiation and, if the system is too chaotic, skills that help unify. But because we're inherently conservative as a species, the great wizards of peace, such as Jesus, carry a sword, not a band-aid. This is why in the creation myth in Genesis the first couple are unceremoniously cast out of their state of perfect harmony. They had eaten the fruit of the tree of life. The fire of evolution had entered them.

Marriage therapists have to make this discernment all the time. A couple might visit a therapist thinking that they just want a little more harmony in their relationship, but a skilful therapist will first help the chaos *deepen*. She will bring fire to bear on the situation. Or, better, she'll create a milieu for the fires of life to burn through the resistance to change. What appears chaotic is actually the life force expressing itself as the need for greater differentiation. The couple can't achieve greater intimacy because they are too close to see each other. They lack perspective. If a therapist thought that her job was to make the relationship more "peaceful," she would be doing a disservice to the evolution of the relationship. To be a peacemaker, more often than not, means being willing to disturb the peace.

We're really conservative as a species. We don't like change. This is true at the level of self, relationships, and social systems. If we can avoid evolving, we will. And it's killing us, quite literally. We're on the brink of another economic crisis, and yet we refuse, because of ideology, to allow our economic system to evolve. We're on the brink of ecological destruction, and yet we refuse to make the shift to a green economy, fund research and development for new technology, consider alternative manufacturing models, and then, as consumers, actually take a chance, for example, on an electric car. We had hoped that the last economic crisis would be profound enough to bring the sword of division between Wall Street and the White House. But the same characters are reading off the same script. We found a way to make peace with the old regime. The crisis that we are facing is nature's way of helping us step outside of how embedded we are in the social, political, economic, and self-systems that do not have sufficient complexity to help us take our next evolutionary step.

Peace It Together is a non-profit organization that brings together Israeli and Palestinian youth so that they can get to know each other as human beings, and not merely as "Israelis" or "Palestinians." The students use film to document the evolution of their relationship with each other. Peace It Together is acting as a peacemaker by providing a safe container for this state of balanced turbulence. The youth are able to step outside of their embedded cultures and differentiate from their inherited ideologies that have defined the "other" as an enemy. And they are also able to deeply bond and make friends with the "enemy." And when they return to their cultures, they will, simply by virtue of their experience, disturb the peace of a status quo that no longer works. May the church be such a container.

Doubting Thomas: Scientific Pioneer

John 20:19-29

Thomas takes a drubbing in John's gospel. The *truly* blessed are those who, unlike poor Thomas, take it on faith that Christ is risen. Thomas, though, is holding out for evidence. Unless he is able to experience Christ for himself, he's not believing it. Tsk, tsk, Thomas. The only evidence a *real* believer needs is the witness of the community of faith. At least, that is the bias of the author of John's gospel, and that's the point he is trying to make with the story in the reading.

But Thomas has a point. Too much is taken on faith—from Jonestown to Waco, Texas, people have been willing to take the word of strong, charismatic leaders and believe pretty much anything, with tragic results.

This is why the scientific method developed in the first place—to tear down the castle of reality as defined, articulated, and defended by vested interests, the church in particular. When Copernicus upset the cosmological apple cart by showing that the sun didn't actually revolve around Earth (it was the other way around, in fact), the church silenced him and his students. Giordano Bruno, a Dominican monk, was burned at the stake, in part for supporting this theory. Galileo was forced to recant what he saw through the lens of his telescope—if you de-centre the Earth, for goodness' sake, what's next? Well, we know what was next. Subsequent generations of the scientific-minded, who were not prepared to take the church's word for it, began to question whether the *church,* never mind the sun, was the centre of the universe. That's when the church authorities felt threatened, and that's when the church got nasty. In the age of reason, any and all claims to truth were tried and tested, not blindly believed because some authority said it was so.

The church has a long history of holding in disdain the likes of Thomas, who want direct and immediate experiences of their faith, unmediated by the power structures of the institution. New Testament scholar Elaine Pagels thinks that the gospel of John was written in part to refute the Gnostic gospel of Thomas.[1] Could this have been the same Thomas referred to in this story from John's gospel? Thomas's gospel is written as a series of sayings of Jesus, and not in narrative form like the New Testament gospels. In Thomas's gospels, Jesus advocates for direct, unbrokered experience of the sacred. He promotes a more mystical theology, in which those with eyes to see don't have to take anybody else's word for it. They can experience the sacred here and now. These are the blessed ones, those who hold out for their own direct experience of the Christ, not those who hear about it from others.

The scientific method is rather straightforward. If you want to know if something is true, develop a hypothesis, create an experiment to test it, and hand over the results to a community of the competent to have a go at it to see if your results are repeatable. Then you have yourself a theory that holds up until someone comes along with a better one. Your theory must be able to be disproved. If it can't be disproved, it won't be taken seriously. You don't take anybody's word for it. You take *nothing* on faith. So Thomas can be considered the protoscientist of the early church. Unless he touches the wounds for himself, he's not going to believe, even if his best friends tell him that it's true. He wants an evidence-based faith.

So, let's get one thing straight: there's nothing about science itself that threatens the church or Christian beliefs. The scientific method is

---

[1] Elaine Pagels, *Beyond Belief: The Secret Gospel of Thomas* (New York: Random House, 2003).

not concerned in the least with proving or disproving the existence of God. As a method of gaining direct knowledge of the physical world, it's brilliant and we have benefited from it in so many ways. The problem is not with the scientific method, it's with a few scientists' assumption—what scholars have called scientism or scientific materialism. This is the assumption that the universe can be reduced to the physical realm, and this is a metaphysical assertion, a belief, not science.

Ever since Darwin, some scientists assume that natural selection is a spirit-less process. Darwin himself may have rejected his Christian faith (the debate is ongoing), and if he did, it was at least partly because he was gobsmacked with wonder at how nature worked. Darwin didn't have any theological models that could accommodate what he was finding. He saw in nature an intrinsic adaptive intelligence bubbling up from within organisms and species. But the way many ecclesiastical authorities saw it was that either God was responsible for creation or nature was, and Darwin's theory of natural selection seemed to elbow out the need for God.

Alfred Wallace Russell, who discovered the mechanism of natural selection at the same time as Darwin, didn't share Darwin's beliefs. He came to the conclusion that natural selection was overseen by a guiding intelligence. Ultimately, science had no need of the hypothesis that the guiding intelligence was God. In fact, science must make the assumption that there are no supernatural forces.

But theology is an interpretive discipline. We may legitimately interpret the findings of science and not be bound to physicalistic explanations of the universe. What if the science of evolution is telling us *how* God brings forth a world? Is it possible that evolution is a divine strategy for world making? Might there be a way to imagine God involved in natural processes in a noncoercive or persuasive way?

The church has inadvertently supported scient*ism* in its predominant theological models. For hundreds of years, mainstream Christians have been taught that God lives *outside* the universe and makes brief forays into this material realm to straighten us out—but then it's back to the extracosmic throne. Most of us have been nurtured on dualism. There are two separate realities—heaven and Earth, spirit and flesh, mind and matter—and mostly they don't have much to do with one another. We handed the material/physical realm over to science, and we kept Spirit, but we've kept the two totally separate. We looked for God outside of time and space. Jesus, our theological models claimed, was the singular incidence of God taking on flesh.

But what if God's radiant occasion of incarnation in the human species through Jesus was part of a pattern and not an exception? Our theological language may need to shift if this is true. We wouldn't talk about *the* incarnation, as though this was the singular incarnational event in the last 13.7 billion years. What if the entire evolutionary process is Spirit growing a body? What if we changed the model and played with the idea that material, physical reality is the outward manifestation of Spirit that is unfolding in an evolutionary universe? Then heaven infuses Earth, spirit animates flesh, and mind can be found within matter. You can distinguish these realms but not absolutely separate them.

The sciences of physics, chemistry, and systems reveal a living universe that knows how to self-renew, self-replicate, and self-organize. What each is touching into, as Thomas touched into Christ's wounded side, is that life just seems to know how to organize into elegant forms. Nobel prize–winning chemist Ilya Prigogine looked at the evidence and came up with the term self-organization.[2] As far as he could tell, self-organization was a fundamental condition of the cosmos: a system under pressure may reorganize itself at a higher level. Galaxies, solar systems, our planet, and all of life, including humans, have a built-in capacity for, and a bias toward, increased complexity, beauty, and consciousness. The intelligence that can pull this off is a standard feature

---

[2] Ilya Prigogine, *Order Out of Chaos: Man's New Dialogue with Nature* (New York: Bantam Books, 1984).

of the universe. We all come equipped with this intelligence.

Chilean biologist Humberto Maturana and the late Francisco Varela, a cognitive scientist, came up with the term *autopoiesis* in 1972.[3] It literally means self-creation. All life—from the cellular level to organs, including our brains—has an in-built capacity to build and regenerate itself.

Physicist David Bohm looked at this phenomenon from the perspective of subatomic physics, where Newtonian physics breaks down and reality is more like a dance, a relationship of probabilities, rather than billiard balls crashing into each other. He noticed an "implicate order," another name for this intelligence at the heart of reality that brings order out of chaos—or rather *is* the implicate order within the chaos.[4] Another name he gave it, which crosses a line into the language of Mystery, is "hidden wholeness."[5] This urge to wholeness moves through every cell and every life form, including you and me. In other words, something lives in the deep within-ness of life that desires maximum self-expression and self-transcendence. Paul says of Christ, "in him all things hold together" (Colossians 1:17), which seems to suggest a similar dynamic in religious language.

You get the picture. The Easter story is not discontinuous with nature. There is what theologian Matthew Fox calls a "natural grace."[6] You can use terms like self-organization, autopoiesis, implicate order, or hidden wholeness. Or you can greet one another in the Easter season with, "Christ is risen!" because Christ is always rising, always becoming manifest in this beautiful, incomprehensible, mysterious world of ours. And you can hold out with Thomas for direct knowledge of Spirit. Start anywhere, go deep, and suspend materialistic assumptions.

---

[3] H.R. Maturana and F.J. Varela, *The Tree of Knowledge: The Biological Roots of Human Understanding* (Boston: Shambhala Publications, 1987).

[4] David Bohm, *Wholeness and the Implicate Order* (London: Routledge, 1980).

[5] F. David Peat and John Briggs, "David Bohm 1917–1992," F. David Peat, January 1987, accessed November 6, 2011, http://fdavidpeat.com/interviews/bohm.htm.

[6] Matthew Fox, *Natural Grace* (New York: Doubleday Press, 1996).

Start with your own life. Start with the fifty trillion cells of your body that are converting energy to make protein right now so that you can read this. Or start with the awareness that the body you are carrying around now won't be the body you'll be carrying around seven years from now—it will have completely rebuilt itself from the inside out. You will have undergone a resurrection of the body. Or start with your own irrepressible urge to be more, to realize the fullness of your potential, or to fashion the best life possible from your precious years on Earth. This is Spirit, raising you up to realize a resurrection, day in and day out.

Spirit is coursing through our very veins. But don't take my word for it, or anybody's word for it. Hold out, with Thomas, for evidence.

The Future Calls

Luke 1:26-38

You'd be perplexed, too, if the angel Gabriel flew into your home one fine afternoon and told you that you had "found favour with God"—perplexed and perhaps a little worried. Because exactly what does it mean to be favoured by God? If you know your Scripture, you'll realize that it's not necessarily the same as drawing the winning number of the Lotto 6/49. Often times, the blessing is deferred so long that God's favoured ones end up scratching their heads and wondering what it must be like to be God's enemy! For instance, Abraham and Sarah are favoured ones, recipients of a different angelic greeting, but by the time Sarah gets around to conceiving, she's putting her teeth in a glass of water before she turns in for the night. Elizabeth conceives John the Baptist only to discover that her son will grow up to join some kind of desert cult and rarely make it home for Hanukkah. Oh sure, the nature of the blessing is clear in hindsight, but don't be fooled: stepping up as a team leader of the God Squad requires courage. No wonder Mary is perplexed when she meets Gabriel.

We're told she took a moment to ponder exactly what this greeting from God's messenger was all about. No kidding! Have you been greeted by any angels lately? Once, when I was in a particularly perplexing stretch of my ministry, I needed a sign and I needed it now. That night, while I was sleeping, I had a dream. A wise older woman approached me and looked carefully all around my face and then asked:

"Do you know that there are angels dancing on your face?" I wanted a big angel, like Gabriel, with wings attached to his back—not these little ones that I couldn't even see. I think the message might have been that I wouldn't know an angel even if an entire squadron were dancing on my face. I, too, pondered the meaning of this greeting. I think the meaning was deep and metaphysical: like, get over yourself!

Of course, hearing that you've been chosen to be the mother of the "Son of the Most High" takes it to a whole new level. In this reflection, I'll explore the spiritual layers of meaning contained in Luke 1:26–38, and do so in a way that we can relate to, even if we have never seen a winged angel in real life.

To do this, we need to assume that this story has meaning that transcends a historical event—that it has *mythic* layers of meaning. That doesn't mean that it's not true. Myths carry meanings that are not limited by history. I don't know what historically happened to Mary. Nobody does. All we have is Luke's account of what happened to Mary, and even if he got every detail right, then the only relevance this story would have for us is whether we believe it or not. Some believe it. Some don't believe it. But believing or not doesn't make much difference to my life today. Myth, on the other hand, allows us to enter the story and experience it for ourselves today.

Mythic stories are timeless—as long as we don't burden them with literalism. Our Christian story of a virgin birth is one of many pagan myths that feature a virgin birth. In fact, scholars are convinced that the writers of the New Testament applied a pre-existing myth of the virgin birth to the story of Jesus.[1] Don't be alarmed. In fact, this liberates us to interpret the story today.

Let's unpack of few of the subversive truths of the myth of Jesus's birth. It's a story about God choosing a Jewish peasant girl from a backwater Galilean village to shape history. There is no doubt in my

---

[1] Tom Harpur, *The Pagan Christ: Recovering the Lost Light* (Toronto: Thomas Allen Publishers, 2005).

mind that the gospel writers were intentionally writing a subversive story about Jesus's beginning. To claim that Mary was the mother of the son of the Most High was to effectively undermine conventional wisdom—namely that the son of the Most High (the historical title for Caesar, Emperor of Rome) was actually born to a peasant woman. It was to claim that God's intention is to shape history through a bunch of powerless people—virtual nobodies in the empire. What does this say about God? Power and status aren't so important to this God. What does it say about the 90% of the population who were lower class? This story lifts up the whole lot of them in first century Mediterranean culture and, by extension, the forgotten ones of the twenty-first century.

This story is so radical that it has taken us two thousand years to catch up. You see, the angel came with news of a possible future scenario. The four major revolutions of the modern era were all about the invisible classes—those relegated to the dustbin of history—rising up. Gandhi's empowerment of the Indian lower classes is a realization of this story of Jesus's conception. A whole new era, marked by the dignity of the forgotten ones, was inaugurated by the consent of a Jewish peasant girl to the promptings of Spirit. History can be interpreted as the slow evolution of humanity agreeing with Mary's yes to the angel Gabriel.

What about the virgin birth? Despite being a mistranslation of a passage from Isaiah that speaks of a "young woman" and not a virgin, this story has stuck. But let's explore it at face value. One of the most subversive meanings is captured in a single line from a Bruce Cockburn Christmas song: "Mary grows a child without the help of a man."[2] The assumptions of patriarchy—that men are the favoured ones, that all good things must happen through the male gender, that men should hold all the power, and that women are naturally subservient— are overturned in this single detail. The virgin birth has nothing to do with concern over sexual impurity. The Jewish tradition affirms the body and sexuality as a gift of God. The myth of the virgin birth is

---

[2] Bruce Cockburn, "Cry of a Tiny Babe," *Nothing But a Burning Light* (Sony, 1991).

announcing the end of one age, patriarchy, and the beginning of a new creation in Christ. To be Christian is to consent to equality. We are now certain that one of the most radical features of the early Christian church was that women enjoyed equal status with men[3]—unheard of anywhere in the world in the first century. It took men in the church a couple of centuries to wrest control back and exclude women. But the story stands in its affirmation that the world can run just fine without the illusion of the necessity of male dominance. In this story, Spirit bypasses patriarchy in the conception and birth of a new humanity, symbolized by the birth of Christ.

Do you see what we miss when we literalize this story and take it at its face value as the historical account of the birth of Christ?

But let's drill down and get a little more personal, shall we? I want you to identify with Mary. Think about the angel in the story as representing the Future. Catholic theologian John Haught thinks about God in this way.[4] All of the yet-unrealized possibilities of the Future come to greet us in our present circumstances, much like the angel greets Mary.

The angels of the Future sometimes greet us as a deep intuition of our own future. When I was a teenager, I snuck off on a Sunday afternoon to listen to William F. Buckley Jr. talk on a TV show. I didn't have a clue what he was talking about, but I loved his use of words and the way he spoke. Is it surprising that I have ended up in a vocation that involves writing and speaking? The Future visited me.

I recently received an email from somebody I didn't know who had a deep desire to do something for the people of Africa. Although I didn't know her, she represented an organization I trusted. She wanted to build forty schools and she was inviting me to donate $100 toward this end. Since I had never met or heard of this woman, this was a

---

[3] Elizabeth Schüssler Fiorenza, *In Memory of Her: A Feminist Theological Reconstruction of Christian Origins* (New York: Crossroad, 1988).

[4] John F. Haught, "Diety," in *Making Sense of Evolution: Darwin, God, and the Drama of Life* (Westminster: John Knox Press, 2011).

strange greeting. The Future was speaking to me in the form of an inner allurement to her cause. What fascinated me about this stranger was that she not only felt compassion for the people of Africa, she had an inner sense that she could make a real difference. A new future could be born through her. She had a Mary-moment and she wanted me to catch the spirit of that moment, which I did and made the donation.

The nine most powerful words in Scripture belong to Mary: "Let it be with me according to your word." Or, more succinctly, "Yes." This single word possesses the power to shape the future. The Christmas story is not something that happened two thousand years ago. It is my story and your story. We're all visited by the presence of the Future, and, yes, it's as strange today as it was for Mary. The future being born through me? Through us? My life as a womb for the birth of the divine? Love taking shape in me? In us? With Mary, we ponder these questions in our hearts. And if we liberate the Christmas story from the tyranny of historical fact, there's much to be gained from this beautiful story.

An Increase in Faith

Luke 17:5-6

Luke 17:5–6 invites us to reflect on the meaning of faith in the twenty-first century. The disciples ask Jesus to "increase our faith." What were they asking for? When we talk about faith *today*, what do we mean? Dr. James Fowler, psychology researcher, wrote a classic called *Stages of Faith*, and his stages correspond rather well with the worldviews that I often use to discuss evolutionary Christianity. With each evolving stage of spiritual development, we could say that there is an increase in faith—that is, there is a development in how we understand faith and how faith functions in our lives.

For many, indeed most, Christians today—and for many atheists—faith is identical to belief. To ask for an increase in faith is to ask for the grace to believe in God more deeply and with more conviction. But even the meaning of "belief in God" evolves depending on your perspective. Although atheists don't believe in God, it always interesting to ask an atheist to tell you about the God they don't believe in. It's a legitimate question, because atheism is not the absence of spiritual intelligence—it is that level of spiritual intelligence at which a person can no longer bring themselves to believe in a *particular* kind of God. Typically, the God they don't believe in is exactly the same God as a believer who is at what Fowler calls the "synthetic-conventional" stage of spiritual development. This God is a cosmic engineer, in absolute charge of history, and everything that happens, happens according to His will (this God is male). He has a plan laid out for all of us. This is pretty much the God that the atheists and many theists share—it's just that one doesn't believe in that God and other does.

The so-called militant atheists today have a mission to eradicate this God from human consciousness. To them, this God is a scourge upon Earth, and the sooner the believers are relieved of their irrational faith, the better off our species will be. Conventional believers, on the other hand, are on a mission to defend this God—sometimes with violence in the case of terrorism. This is a clash between a traditional/mythic worldview and the modernist worldview. For the record, if I were forced to choose between conventional belief in this kind of God and the atheists' rejection of this God, I'd go with atheism. I don't believe in a God who controls history or who intervenes in human affairs to rescue us—or, indeed, for reasons that are mysterious to us, refuses to intervene in the most desperate of circumstances.

Thankfully, I'm not forced to choose. I have no truck with modernist atheism, either. I regard it is a form of spiritual intelligence that got frozen and needs to evolve. The proof that it needs to evolve is that it is incessantly trying to eradicate a God that has already died, many times, in the last fifty years. In a CBC radio interview with Jian Ghomeshi, Deepak Chopra asked how often that God has to die. I'm not even interested in the project of killing off that God. It still serves many good people to believe in that God, and I don't see any compelling reason to destroy their belief. (Although we do need to defend ourselves against the violence it can engender.) These atheist scientists are serving an important function in their attempt to bring reason and the empirical method to bear on the orientation that we might call "faith as believing the right things" about God. But I do wish that they would awaken to the possibility that there are higher forms of spiritual intelligence than both the traditional faith-as-right belief and modernist atheism.

It's actually becoming tedious. Take, for example, the novel *36 Arguments for the Existence of God*, which should have been entitled 36

Arguments *Against* the Existence of God. It was written by Rebecca Newberger Goldstein, PhD (Stanford), a philosopher and novelist who is married to Steve Pinker, an avowed atheist scientist himself. It is well written, and witty, but in the end, it's all too predictable. Every character that is rational, balanced, and possessing integrity is represented by secular atheist humanists. The wing nuts, the irrational, and the regressive are all believers. The climax of the novel is a debate between a Harvard philosopher and an economist, who is a traditional Christian and whose arguments for the existence of God are pathetic and tired. Atheism trounces conventional faith. Yawn.

Let's shift gears then. Jesus's response to the disciples' request for an increase in faith is, "If you had faith the size of a mustard seed, you could say to this mulberry tree, 'Be uprooted and planted in the sea,' and it would obey you." He doesn't talk about believing more, believing harder, believing better, or believing at all. His response has nothing to do with belief. It focuses on agency—faith as the power to accomplish something, even the impossible.

From an evolutionary perspective, faith as agency develops.

From a traditional perspective (the conventional stage of faith), the mantra is, "God can do it." No matter how bad things get, God will come through in the end. No matter what you are going through, God will make it better. No matter the obstacle, God can overcome it. God is all-powerful, all-knowing, and all-beneficent. All you need to do is to put your trust in God's agency. So, when we are functioning from this wave of consciousness, when Jesus says that even mulberry bushes will obey our commands, we hear something close to: "God can do it, because God can do anything." But it's God's agency, not our own, that is at play. What we need to do is surrender our own power, and then God's power will kick in and accomplish what we cannot.

Well, that worked right up until about five hundred years ago, when it first dawned on human consciousness that this was a rather passive stance, which is the downside of this traditional worldview. If it's all unfolding according to God's plan, then I can just sit back and trust God—or God's representatives, the king or queen, the church and her priests, the aristocracy, or whoever is the reigning authority— to run the show. There is a potential for acquiescence to the status quo, on both a political and personal level: It's all God's will. I just need to believe it more, especially when things don't go my way.

When the modernist worldview, or what Claire Graves called the achievist worldview,[1] emerged five hundred years ago, it dawned on humans that we had tremendous unrealized potential. We discovered agency to create a brave new world. At first, there was room for God in this worldview. But this was God as the First Cause, the Divine Principle that got the whole thing started. After that, He let us and natural laws run the show. Today, scientists who have faith in God tend to be Deists—the belief system associated with modernism. God is the watchmaker who got the whole thing going, but then He lets it run itself and never tinkers. Indeed, during the last three hundred years, and in particular in the last sixty years, there has been an unparalleled liberation of human potential. Advances in science, technology, medicine, and how we think have been enormous.

The mantra of modernism as it relates to our theme of faith as agency is: "I can do it." If it sounds a bit like that development stage of a child who demands that his or her agency be honoured, "No, I can do it *myself*," that's because there is an element of that in the modernist worldview. Along with all the dignities associated with this unleashing of human potential in the modern period, we are well aware of the disasters: technology applied to nuclear weapons, the downside of fossil fuel consumption, enormous and unsustainable disparities in wealth, and rampant individualism.

Most associate the modern period with secular humanism and the loss of faith. But it's possible to reimagine modernity as a shift

---

[1] Don Edward Beck and Christopher C. Cowan, *Spiral Dynamics: Mastering Values, Leadership, and Change* (Oxford: Blackwell Publishing, 1996), 244–259.

in where we locate faith—away from a supernatural Being and toward the individual. If we conceive of faith the way Jesus apparently did (as the power to transform present circumstances into a desired future), then the modern worldview, with its rejection of a sky God, is a step forward in the evolution of faith and not the absence of it. Modernism is faith in human potential. When the modernist hears Jesus's teaching in Luke 17:5–6, she might think: "Well, it's true: We can walk on the moon. We can split the atom. We've eradicated many diseases. We can make deserts bloom. Moving a tree is nothing. But I don't need God to do it. I can do it."

The worldview to emerge out of modernism is postmodernism and the rise of empathic consciousness. This structure of consciousness was present in pockets throughout the modern period (particularly the Romantic poets), but it really began to gel in the 1960s. This worldview is, in a way, reactionary. It's a reaction to the indignities of the modern period—the excessive rationalism, the grand narratives of history told through the perspective of the dominant power, the luxurious lifestyles of some when there is so much poverty, the pollution, the extinction of species, and the indignities of the Industrial Revolution.

The religious postmodernists live out their faith through the power of the collective. Modernity's hard-won gains for the dignity of the individual are not lost. But whatever we intend to accomplish must be for the good of everybody, not just the few. We are co-creators with God of a more just, compassionate, and egalitarian society. God returns to the scene after modernism, but this is a God with a heart, a God who is more inclusive, who doesn't take sides, who affirms all religious faiths as equal—a sensitive and empathic God who doesn't so much control history as suffer it with us. God is more like a comrade in the battle against the indignities of modernism than She is a supernatural being to be feared and obeyed. The mantra of postmodernist faith is: "Together, with God as our co-creator, we work for the good of all." The people emerge as the third superpower, and authority is shared and exercised through grassroots movements.

Faith does, in fact, increase in the sense that it becomes a more complex and nuanced expression of life in God. "God alone can do it" morphs into "I can do it" with or without God, which gives rise to "We can do it with our co-creator, God."

The next evolution in our yearning to increase our faith is charac-terized first by recognizing that all of these faith orientations are true but partial. Many of us are composites of each of these orientations: if we're in a twelve-step program, we know the power of trusting in a Higher Power to accomplish what we've been unable to accomplish (the traditional, premodern worldview); if we've been touched by the human potential movement that started in the 60s, if we own a suc-cessful business, or if we are elite athletes, we know about our own potential to accomplish great things (modern); if we've been in the United Church for a few years, then we also know about the convic-tion that together with our co-creator, God, we can change the system for the betterment of all—the voice of the labour movement is heard, women get equal pay for equal work, gays and lesbians acquire the legal right to marry (postmodern). Most of us slide easily between these faith orientations as we consider how to best make a difference in the world. At this emergent stage of faith, we lose the need to deni-grate other expressions of faith.

This integral wave of consciousness is just now emerging on Earth, so it's more difficult to capture it in a pithy mantra. My initial stab at a mantra for what might simply be called the evolutionary stage of faith would be something like "the future is in us." We are, collectively and individually, conscious centres of the singular, evolving Reality. Reality is the interfusion of Spirit, Cosmos, Earth, and the human species evolving toward deeper, livelier, zestier expressions of Love and Cre-ativity. Each part is an expression of a unified whole. We are the fruit of a primal seed that is now realizing its inner potential. The future is in us, but at this stage, we realize this out of a dramatically expanded context and sense of purpose than we enjoyed in the modernist period. It's not about us. It's about the advance of Love.

What is the increase in faith that we are called to undergo today? Jesus uses the metaphor of the mustard seed, which is apt in that it's so small and seemingly insignificant—the way many of us feel—and yet it is power-packed with dormant potential. Faith the size of a mustard seed, Jesus tells the disciples, has power to accomplish the "impossible." Just as a tiny mustard seed contains the entire DNA of its species, we are the seeds that contain the image of God as Love and Creativity. We are stamped with this divine image, and within us is the entire blueprint of the universe, the Earth, and the human species. Under the right conditions, the hard shell that keeps that potential both protected and locked down will break open, and we will realize our potential as centres of the emerging future.

Faith, in this sense, is closer to a knowing—what the ancients called gnosis—than it is to a belief in anything. The power of a seed doesn't lie in what it believes. Neither does a seed will a new future into existence. It *is* the future—present in all its dormant potential— waiting to be released. Plant yourself in the right conditions: a community to help you remember this expansive identity, the capacity to ponder mystery, a regular spiritual practice of reorienting yourself in this bigger identity, and consciously imagining yourself becoming the presence of Love and Creativity in your daily life. These conditions are the nutrients that will crack open the shell and release the latent potential within the seed.

Faith becomes more of a verb than a noun. As dynamic centres of Creativity and Love, we "faith" new futures into reality.

This is what I think Jesus was trying to do when he talked about the mustard seed—to reorient the disciples as seeds who possess, in their very natures, the power and potential of the whole of Reality as Sacred Mystery. The various crises facing us as a species right now may represent a set of necessary conditions—the nutrients, if you like—for this personal and collective breaking open and tapping into our deepest potential. Ecological degradation, climate change, species extinction, terrorism, poverty, and loveless relationships are catalysts in the evocation of new intelligences, including spiritual intelligence. They are cracking us open, causing us to re-examine who we think we are and what this life is for, so that the life within the seed may be released.

Many look out at the world and conclude that it's impossible at this point to do anything about it—that it's too late. But, as Paul writes, with God, "all things are possible" (Matthew 19:26). God here is the Sacred Mystery comprising an intuition that an intelligent power and a loving presence is active in the world, noncoercively weaving patterns from the apparent chaos, wooing us to fall back in love with each other and Earth. But more than this, we begin to awaken to the possibility that we are an occasion of that same power and presence. Our lives are the presence of Sacred Mystery yearning for flesh-and-blood expression. We see that in how we live each moment, in the choice to open our hearts to love when instinctively we want to close them, or when we open our ears to listen when we just want to speak *our* truth, or when we allow compassion to flood through us. In these moments, we are the future present. Our lives become both a glimpse of what is possible and an evocation of the same Sacred Mystery we've been waiting for all our lives. We are seeds of Sacred Mystery, evolutionary mystics, centres of that ever-emerging future Jesus called the Kin(g) dom of God.

Bibliography

Baron-Cohen, Simon. *The Science of Evil: On Empathy and the Origins of Cruelty*. New York: Basic Books, 2001.

Beck, Don Edward, and Christopher C. Cowan. Version *Spiral Dynamics: Mastering Values, Leadership, and Change*. Oxford: Blackwell Publishing, 1996.

Benyus, Janine. *Biomimicry: Innovation Inspired by Nature*. New York: Harper Perennial, 1997.

Bohm, David. *Wholeness and the Implicate Order*. London: Routledge, 1980.

Caputo, John D. *The Weakness of God: A Theology of the Event*. Bloomington: Indiana University Press, 2006.

Church, Russell. "Emotional Reactions of Rats to the Pain of Others." *Journal of Comparative and Physiological Psychology* 52, 1959.

Cockburn, Bruce. "Cry of a Tiny Babe." *Nothing But a Burning Light*. Sony, 1991.

Cohen, Andrew. "The Mythic Life and Times of Deepak Chopra." *EnlightenNext magazine*. May–July 2008. http://www.enlightennext.org/magazine/j40/chopra.asp?.

Crossan, John Dominic. *The Birth of Christianity: Discovering What Happened in the Years Immediately After the Execution of Jesus*. New York: HarperCollins Publishers, 1998.

Darwin, Charles. *On the Origin of Species by Means of Natural Selection*. New York: D. Appleton and Company, 1870.

Dawkins, Richard. *The God Delusion*. Boston: Houghton Mifflin Harcourt, 2006.

Dictionary.com. *Online Etymology Dictionary*. Accessed November 6, 2011. http://dictionary.reference.com/browse/reconcile.

Dowd, Michael. *Thank God for Evolution: How the Marriage of Science and Religion Will Transform Your Life and Our World*. Toronto: Penguin Group, 2007.

Eldredge, Niles, and S.J. Gould. "Punctuated Equilibria: an Alternative to Phyletic Gradualism." In N. Eldredge, *Time Frames*. Princeton: Princeton University Press, 1985.

Elgin, Duane. *The Living Universe: Where Are We? Who Are We? Where Are We Going?* San Francisco: Berrett-Koehler Publishers, Inc., 2009.

Fowler, James W. *Stages of Faith: The Psychology of Human Development and the Quest for Meaning.* New York: HarperCollins Publishers, 1981.

Fox, Matthew. *Natural Grace.* New York: Doubleday Press, 1996.

Hafiz. "Look! I Am a Whale." *The Gift: Poems by Hafiz, the Great Sufi Master.* Trans. Daniel Ladinsky. Toronto: Penguin Group, 1999.

Hamilton, Marilyn. *Integral City: Evolutionary Intelligences for the Human Hive.* Gabriola Island: New Society Publishers, 2008.

Harpur, Tom. *The Pagan Christ: Recovering the Lost Light.* Toronto: Thomas Allen Publishers, 2005.

Haught, John. *God After Darwin: A Theology of Evolution.* Philadelphia: Westview Press, 2008.

———. "Diety." *Making Sense of Evolution: Darwin, God, and the Drama of Life.* Westminster: John Knox Press, 2011.

Hawken, Paul, Amory B. Lovins, and Hunter L. Lovins. *Natural Capitalism: The Next Industrial Revolution.* Washington, DC: Earthscan LLC, 2010.

Hawking, Stephen, and Leonard Mlodinow. *The Grand Design.* New York: Bantam Books, 2010.

Heschel, Abraham Joshua. *God in Search of Man: A Philosophy of Judaism.* Toronto: Douglas & McIntyre Ltd., 1983.

Hitchens, Christopher. *God Is Not Great: How Religion Poisons Everything.* Toronto: McClelland and Stewart, 2007.

Hopkins, Gerard Manley. "God's Grandeur." *God's Grandeur and Other Poems.* Toronto: General Publishing Company, Ltd., 1995.

Kegan, Robert. *The Evolving Self: Problem and Process in Human Development.* Cambridge: Harvard University Press, 1982.

King, Barbara J. *Evolving God: A Provocative View on the Origins of Religion.* New York: Doubleday, 2007.

Macaulay, Thomas Babingon. *Critical and Historical Essays Contributed to "The Edinburgh Review."* London: Longman, Brown, Greens, and Longmans, 1850.

Maturana, H.R., and F.J. Varela. *The Tree of Knowledge: The Biological Roots of Human Understanding.* Boston: Shambhala Publications, 1987.

McDonough, William, and Michael Braungart. *Cradle to Cradle: Remaking the Way We Make Things.* New York: North Point Press, 2002.

McFague, Sallie. *The Body of God: An Ecological Theology.* Minneapolis: Fortress Press, 1993.

McIntosh, Steve. *Integral Consciousness and the Future of Evolution: How the Integral Worldview Is Transforming Politics, Culture and Spirituality.* New York: Continuum, 2007.

Monbiot, George. "Matt Ridley's Rational Optimist is Telling the Rich What They Want to Hear." *The Guardian.* June 18, 2010. http://guardian.co.uk/commentisfree/cif-green/2010/jun/18/matt-ridley-rational-optimist-errors?INTCMP=SRCH.

On Truth & Reality. Accessed November 20, 2011. http://spaceandmotion.com/physics-quantum-bohmian-mechanics.htm.

Newberger Goldstein, Rebecca. *36 Arguments for the Existence of God: A Work of Fiction.* New York: Pantheon Books, 2010.

Pagels, Elaine. *Beyond Belief: The Secret Gospel of Thomas.* New York: Random House, 2003.

Palmer, Parker J. *Let Your Life Speak: Listening for the Voice of Vocation.* San Francisco: Jossey-Bass, 2000.

Peat, David F., and John Briggs. "David Bohm 1917–1992." F. David Peat, January 1987. Accessed November 6, 2011. http://fdavidpeat.com/interviews/bohm.htm.

Prigogine, Ilya. *Order Out of Chaos: Man's New Dialogue with Nature.* New York: Bantam Books, 1984.

The Rational Optimist. Accessed February 19, 2012. http://rationaloptimist.com/cv

Ridley, Matt. *The Rational Optimist: How Prosperity Evolves.* New York: HarperCollins Publishers, 2010.

Rifkin, Jeremy. *The Empathic Civilization: The Race to Global Consciousness in a World of Crisis.* New York: Penguin Group Inc., 2009.

Schüssler Fiorenza, Elisabeth. *In Memory of Her: A Feminist Theological Reconstruction of Christian Origins.* New York: Crossroad, 1988.

"Secretary-General's remarks at the ringing of the Peace Bell for the International Day of Peace." September 20, 2002. The United Nations Secretary-General's Statements. Accessed November 13, 2011. http://www.un.org/apps/sg/sgstats.asp?nid=71.

Simmons, Gary. *The I of the Storm: Embracing Conflict, Creating Peace.* Wellington: Unity Books, 2001.

Swimme, Brian. *The Hidden Heart of the Cosmos: Humanity and the New Story.* New York: Orbis Books, 1996.

Teilhard de Chardin, Pierre. *Christianity and Evolution: Reflections on Science and Religion.* Trans. Rene Hague. New York: Harcourt, Brace and Co., 1969.

———. *The Phenomenon of Man.* Harper Perennial: New York, 1955.

Tillich, Paul. *The Eternal Now.* New York: Charles Scribner's Songs, 1963.

"The United Church at 100 in 2 Minutes and 25 Seconds – Revised." YouTube video. Posted by davidewart1945. May 7, 2009. http://www.youtube.com/watch?v=BF4LMiqc370.

Visser, Margaret. *Beyond Fate.* Toronto: House of Anansi Press, 2002.

"Where is Away?" YouTube video. Posted by feelgoodworld. August 31, 2010. http://www.youtube.com/watch?v=UJARRREipmI.

Whitehead, A.N. *Adventures of Ideas.* Toronto: The Free Press, 1967.

Wilber, Ken. *Sex, Ecology, Spirituality: The Spirit of Evolution.* Boston: Shambala Publications, Inc., 2000.

———. *Up From Eden: A Transpersonal View of Human Evolution.* Garden City, NY: Anchor Press/Doubleday, 1981.

Further Reading

Cohen, Andrew. *Evolutionary Enlightenment: A New Path to Spiritual Awakening.* New York: Select Books, 2011.

De Waal, Frans. *The Age of Empathy.* Toronto: McClelland and Stewart, 2009.

Delio, Ilia. *Christ in Evolution.* New York: Orbis Books, 2008.

Roughgarden, Joan. *The Genial Gene: Deconstructing Darwinian Selfishness.* Berkeley: University of California Press, 2009.

Moltmann, Jurgen. *A Theology of Hope.* Harper and Row: New York, 1965.

Swimme, Brian. *The Universe Is a Green Dragon.* Bear and Company, 1984.

Wilber, Ken. *Integral Spirituality: A Startling New Role for Religion in the Modern and Postmodern World.* Boston: Integral Books, 2006.

Bruce Sanguin grew up in Winnipeg and spent his teens and early twenties as a jock. He graduated from the University of Winnipeg having read, as far as he can remember, only one book, a book by Maharishi Mahesh Yogi on Transcendental Meditation. This woke him up to a vocation that transcended the dream of dunking the b-ball and playing professional tennis. Transcendental Meditation gave way to born-again Christianity, then to liberal Christianity and then the total loss of conviction (they are connected), and then to evolutionary Christian mysticism and the blessed return of enthusiasm. Bruce has been an ordained minister in the United Church of Canada for twenty-six years, now serving the Canadian Memorial United Church in Vancouver, B.C. He is a clinical member of the American Association of Marriage and Family Therapy. He's also a husband to Ann (twenty-five years and counting), a father to Sarah (an actress and musician in LA), a grandfather to four, and the author of five books that are all available in both digital and hardcopy from his website: IfDarwinPrayed.com.

When we awake
sometimes we do
not know the country
where we find ourselves.

CPSIA information can be obtained at www.ICGtesting.com
Printed in the USA
LVOW060533150512

281695LV00002B/4/P

9 780986 592430